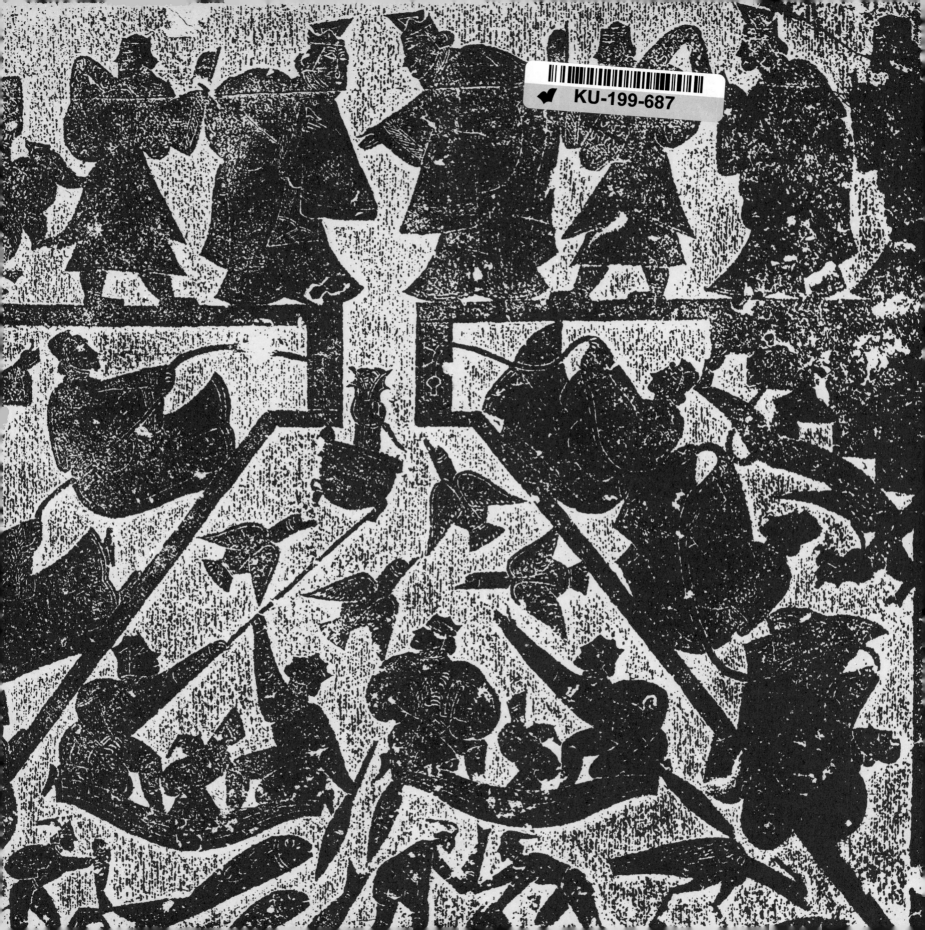

THE FIRST EMPEROR OF CHINA

THE FIRST EMP

秦始皇

EROR OF CHINA

R.W.L. GUISSO
CATHERINE PAGANI
with DAVID MILLER

In association with The National Film Board of Canada and
The Canadian Museum of Civilization
and The Xi'an Film Studio

A Literary Management Group Book

Stoddart

A Literary Management Group Book

Conceived, edited and designed by
The Literary Management Group Inc.
1250 Bay Street, Suite 400
Toronto, Ontario, M5R 2B1
Canada

Publisher: Allan J. Stormont
Editor: Colleen Dimson
Designer: Fortunato Aglialoro
(Falcom Design & Communications Inc.)
Calligrapher: Charles Wing-Hoi Chan
Picture Editor: Catherine Pagani

Published in Canada, 1989 by Stoddart Publishing Co. Limited
34 Lesmill Road
Toronto, Canada M3B 2T6

CANADIAN CATALOGUING IN PUBLICATION DATA

Guisso, R.W.L.
The First Emperor of China

ISBN 0-7737-2370-6
1. Qin Shihuang, Emperor of China, 259-210 B.C.
2. China – History, Qin Dynasty, 221-210 B.C.
3. China – Kings and rulers – Biography 1. Title
I. Pagani, Catherine. II. Miller, David, 1944
D 5747 9. C47C85 1989 931'.04'0924 C89-094455-5

Printed and Bound in Canada
Typesetting: PrimeType Inc., Toronto, Canada
Origination: Colour Technologies, Toronto, Canada
Printing: Ashton-Potter Limited, Toronto, Canada
Binding: T.H. Best Printing Company, Toronto, Canada

Acknowledgements

WE WOULD LIKE TO THANK the following for their generous time, expertise, patience and many intangible contributions to this project in unusual and sometimes trying times.

The National Film Board of Canada, in particular Colin Neale and to Margaret Wong for an outstanding effort; The Canadian Museum of Civilization; The China Film Coproduction Corporation; China Xi'an Film Studios; Doris Dohrenwend, Sara Irwin, Barbara Stephen and Jack Howard of the Far Eastern Department of the Royal Ontario Museum; Mr. John Summers and Mr. B. Cocchiola; Philippa Lewis of London, England for some absolutely intrepid research; Mr. Dan Mokich of the Department of External Affairs, Ottawa for his interest and generous help; and finally to Herb Hilderley and to Howard Albert each for their individual roles in helping develop the project in early days.

CONTENTS 内容

INTRODUCTION
8

GUIDE TO
PRONOUNCIATION
9

Part One
LIKE
A TIGER
OR A WOLF

The Life and Deeds
of Qin Shihuang
10

Part Two
THE LAND
OF HUNGRY
GHOSTS

Warfare in
Ancient China
40

Part Three
ALL
UNDER
HEAVEN

The Unification
of China
82

Part Four

THE EMPEROR AND HIS BLACKHAIRED PEOPLE

Life in the Qin Dynasty

112

Part Five

THE DEATH OF THE PRIMAL DRAGON

The Fall of the Qin Dynasty

158

Part Six

TEN THOUSAND GENERATIONS

The Legacy of Qin Shihuang

190

BACKGROUND

209

FUTURE READING

211

ILLUSTRATION & PHOTO CREDITS

212

INDEX

214

Introduction

AS THIS BOOK WAS going to press in the early Summer of 1989, events as remarkable as those recorded in these pages were again taking place in China. Extraordinarily noble crowds of people in Beijing's Tiananmen Square were calling for unprecedented, yet basic, human rights in the most unique and dramatic way.

The students of Tiananmen Square seemed to be writing history in a manner as large as their First Emperor Qin Shihuang did more than two thousand years ago – as this time they engaged and galvanized a watching world using the 20th century's electronic media.

The leadership of The People's Republic appeared to be retreating to the same secrecy as the First Emperor himself had employed in the face of unparallelled threats.

And so, as contemporary China changes and the secrets of its ancient past are being slowly revealed, the interest in this vast nation and its extraordinary past has never been higher.

In a quite unexpected way then, The First Emperor of China presents a most uncannily relevant portrait of the nature of China and its approach to people and government – then and now.

Events will most certainly have raced on and changed China in probably quite radical ways before you the reader will hold these stories of its great First Emperor – however we hope that we have provided you an entertaining and useful guide to some of the history of this most fascinating nation.

This book presents the story of The First Emperor of China – a man who must be considered remarkable by any standards of any period in human history. Until fifteen years ago, the name of China's First Emperor was unknown in the West. In spite of his towering achievements, his historical notoriety among the Chinese, and a legacy still prominent in China today, he has long remained a shadowy figure, a cypher and a symbol shrouded in the mists of time. Only with the discovery of his tomb in 1974, along with the army of life-size terracotta soldiers which stands guard over it, have the mists parted to reveal something of the man who, for 2200 years, has been hidden within them: Qin Shihuang – First Sovereign Emperor of China.

Few visitors to the world's most populous nation can remain unaware of his works for long. The emperor's legacy surrounds us all, whether we marvel in astonishment at the architectural feat known as the Great Wall, or gaze in wonder upon row after row of his exquisitely-detailed terracotta soldiers. The magnificence of the Forbidden City in Beijing, we are reminded, pales before the fabled splendours of Shihuang's palaces. And as we travel the system of roads and canals which he began, or hold in our hands the coins he made standard, we are reminded of this remarkable ruler. The script we see all around us, in newspapers and on shop-signs, traces its form to his rule. He was a man of "firsts," and in a real sense, the maker of China.

For the past 150 years China has suffered much. Humiliated by Western imperialism throughout the nineteenth century, and subjected to warlordism, foreign invasion, civil war and mass revolutionary movements in the twentieth, the people of the Middle Kingdom have known little peace. Even today, their struggle for modernization and for the "democratization" of their political system is a turbulent one. And the people of China are looking now to the rest of the world, seeking to define their role in it. We in the West, have a duty to understand.

In the twentieth century, Western views of China have varied from puzzlement to pity, from fear to scorn, and only rarely do they include admiration. Yet, historically, China has been a donor civilization, enriching the culture of the whole world with her science and technology, her arts and her philosophy. She still has much to contribute. The achievements of the First Emperor are not just the dusty monuments of a long-dead past. They symbolize, rather, the heights reached in his own time by those whom he called the "Blackhaired people," and the heights once more within their reach.

This work is a modest step in the direction of greater mutual understanding.

R.W.L. Guisso
June 1, 1989

Guide to Pronunciation

The romanization of the Chinese language used in this book follows the *pinyin* system which is now the official phonetic system of Mainland China. Each character is rendered into one syllable. The pronunciation of the letters used in this system does not always follow those to which Westerners are accustomed. The following list is a rough guide to the most unusual of these.

Initials

c	is pronounced as *ts* in 'cats'
j	is pronounced like *g* in 'gem'
q	is pronounced like *ch*, but is strongly aspirated
r	is pronounced like *su* in 'measure'
x	is an aspirated sound somewhat equivalent to *sh*
z	is pronounced as *ds* in 'seeds'
zh	is pronounced as *j* in 'joy'

Finals

i	is pronounced as *ee* in 'see'
o	is pronounced as *o* in 'stop'
u	is similar to the French *u* sound
ai	is pronounced as *igh* in 'high'
an	is pronounced as *an* in 'tan'
ou	is pronounced as *o* in 'no'
ui	is pronounced as *ay* in 'stay'
ang	the *a* has the sound of *a* in 'father'
eng	is pronounced as *ung* in 'rung'
ong	the *o* is somewhat similar to *ow* in 'own'
chi shi zhi	in these three syllables, the final *i* is pronounced as *er* in 'her'

For example, the name of the First Emperor, Qin Shihuang, is pronounced as 'Chin Sher-huang.' His tomb mound is located near present-day Xi'an, pronounced 'Shee-an.'

O*n the title page of the book, Qin Shihuang's seal is written in an unusual style of Chinese characters called "bird script."*

T*he illustrations used for the endpapers and the section openers are rubbings made by the eminent sinologist Edouard Chavannes of Han dynasty stone pillars from the Wu family tomb. These rubbings, made in the early part of this century, show lively depictions of various stories and legends from China's past.*

A*long with the English titles for each section of the book, the Chinese characters have also been provided.*

T*he ancient Chinese character for "page" has been placed with each page number of the book.*

画像

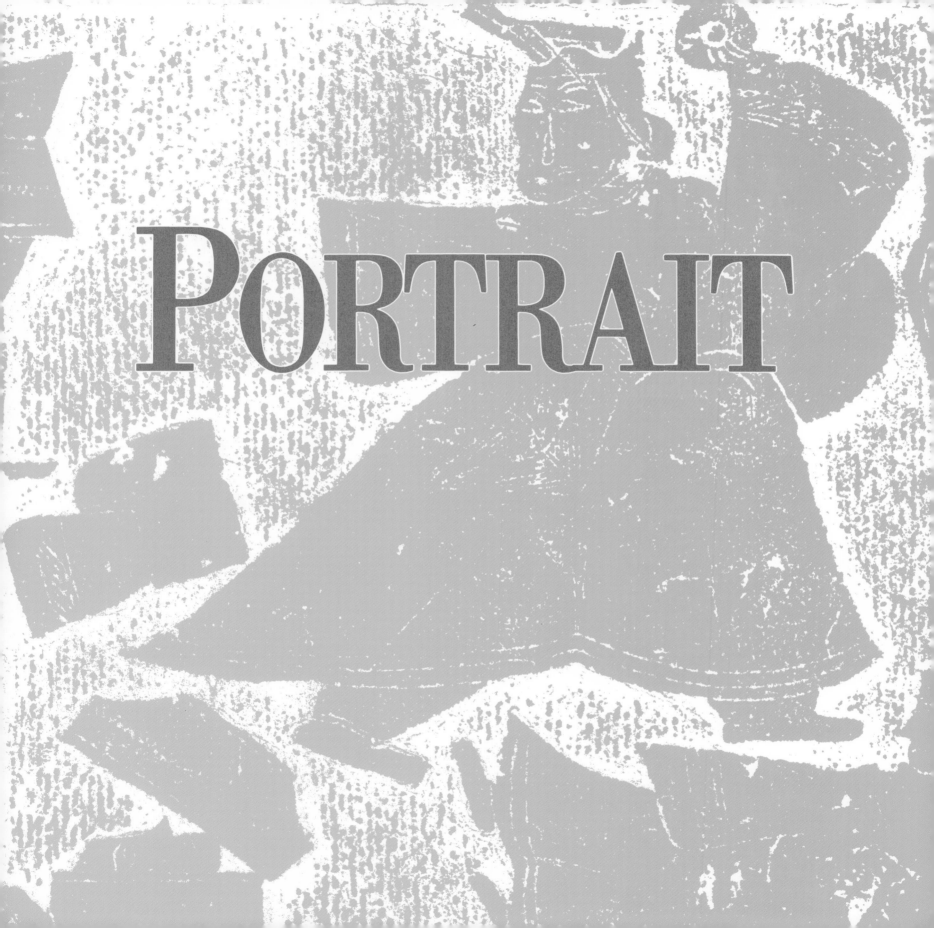

PORTRAIT

LIKE A TIGER OR A WOLF

The Life and Deeds of Qin Shihuang

Demon or Demi-God?

IT WAS A TIME OF ENDLESS WARS and constant death when Qin Shihuang was born in 259 B.C. The bastard son of a treacherous merchant, he would become the founder of China, but at his birth, the feudal land he would one day rule was torn apart by savage battles, and the peasants' lives were filled with wretchedness. Under Qin Shihuang's rule, much of his people's misery would end, but the First Emperor's methods of achieving peace and prosperity would make him, even to this day, the subject of fierce division among the world's historians.

Was he a demon or demi-god? they argued. A visionary or despot? A tyrant who rode his fabled six white horses over the back of millions of peasants, or a benevolent ruler who truly cared about the fate of his people?

To begin, he was the First Emperor of China — the first in the long line of 210 men and one woman to occupy the Dragon Throne before its collapse in 1911. In fact, the very word "emperor" (*huangdi*) we owe to Qin Shihuang, and it is from the name of his dynasty called Qin (pronounced "Chin") that we are given the word for the country we call China. He was also a visionary who united the Warring States of his time, imposed order and conformity upon them, and so founded China's 2200-year-old Imperial System — the longest-enduring of all human political systems.

One of the most amazing rulers of all time, Qin Shihuang was a conqueror, a unifier, a centralizer, a standardizer, a builder — and a destroyer. If we sought in Western history, men of comparable achievement, it is the names of Alexander the Great, (356-323 B.C.) and Julius Caesar, (100-44 B.C.) that most readily come to mind.

Why is it, then, that from the time of his death the historians of Imperial China have vilified his memory?

He "cracked his great whip to bend the world to his will," and "placed deceit and violence above kindness and justice, making tyranny the foundation of his Empire." These are the words of his earliest critic, a scholar called Jia Yi whose famous essay "The Sins of Qin" was written shortly after the fall of the Qin dynasty. Few scholars have disputed this judgement until recent years, and it was not until Mao Tse-tung expressed his admiration both for the success and ruthlessness of the First Emperor that widespread reappraisal began.

In 1958 at a meeting of the Central Committee of the Chinese Communist Party, Chairman Mao remarked that Qin Shihuang was a ruler who advocated the extermination of those who "used the past to criticize the present." Mao went on to say, "What does he amount to anyway? He buried only 460 scholars alive, while we have buried 46,000 counter revolutionary scholars alive."

In response to Mao's remarks, highly favorable and basically uncritical biographies of Shihuang began to appear from 1972 in China where they sold in editions numbering in the millions. It was exactly the kind of mass mobilization that the First Emperor would have approved of and understood!

Tyrannical or enlightened ruler? Deliverer of his people, or oppressor? Princely son of a king, or illegitimate child of a contemptible merchant? The polarization of historical opinion can both illuminate and obscure the facts of a ruler's life, so let us re-examine his accomplishments and see what conclusions we can draw from the life and deeds of China's First Emperor.

The adulation of Qin Shihuang by Chinese historians began after an unsuccessful attempt on the life of Chairman Mao Tse-tung in September of 1971. According to documents later released, his enemies had referred to Mao as a "feudal tyrant" and "a contemporary Qin Shihuang." His supporters then mounted a nation-wide campaign to show that Shihuang had been an enlightened ruler whose greatest achievement was, like Mao's, the unification of China. Numerous books and articles on Shihuang appeared in a short space of time and formed the basis for discussion meetings throughout the country. The most widely-distributed was a biography of the First Emperor by Hong Shidi. The initial printing of this work, in May of 1972, was 1.3 million copies and in just over a year, there were over 2 million copies in print!

This rubbing was made from a roof tile end from the palace of the First Emperor.

秦始皇像

The First Emperor, Qin Shihuang.

The Great Unifier

ALTHOUGH RELIABLE DETAILS about the life of the First Emperor are sketchy, we do know that he was born in 259 B.C. and died in 210 B.C. after twenty-nine years of rule, first as King Zheng of Qin, and then as Shihuang, the "First Emperor" of the Qin dynasty. However, it is by the name of Qin Shihuang that he is known to history, and when one considers the short time he lived and reigned, his accomplishments seem even more astounding than at first glance.

He was only thirteen years old when he ascended to the throne of the state of Qin in 246 B.C., and the country of China did not yet exist. At that time Qin was merely one of seven warring states vying for control of the Central Plain in what seemed a never-ending series of bloody and corrosive battles.

After a period of eight years, while his mother, a one-time courtesan who had become dowager queen, and Lu Buwei, the court advisor, rumored to be her lover and Shihuang's real father, acted as regents for the boy king, Shihuang donned the cap and sword of his majority in 238 B.C.

Now that he had reached the age of twenty-one, it became obvious that Shihuang had learned more under his mentors than even they had suspected. Informed of a plot to rebel against him masterminded by the ambitious and disloyal Lu Buwei, Shihuang, swiftly and without qualms, disgraced his chief advisor and then forced him to commit suicide. He then immediately raised up a new advisor in his place, and together with this man, Li Si, who during his twenty years with Shihuang rose to the highest position in the land, Chancellor of the Left, the young king set out to unify the land.

Firmly Shihuang took control, directing the expert diplomacy and the careful formation of alliances which led to his brilliant success in the brutal unification wars that dominated the history of that period in the 220s. After five centuries of disunity and strife in the land, Shihuang had succeeded in what no ruler before him had been able to accomplish: The country was united and the Qin dynasty proclaimed in 221 B.C. It had taken Shihuang only twenty-five years to accomplish his goal of becoming the First and August Emperor of a vast and undivided land.

Li Si, the advisor who had succeeded Lu Buwei, was later to make the misleading remark that the power of the new emperor had prevailed as easily "as sweeping dust from the kitchen stove." Yet when we learn from the traditional historical sources of the time that the casualties during this period come to over a million deaths, we can see that Li Si's statement was made to flatter his emperor rather than reveal the truth about the costs involved.

Although Shihuang had only eleven more years to live after founding his dynasty, under his rule a total transformation of the land we now call China took place. He created new administrative units for the capital city of Xianyang and the rest of the country, he abolished the feudal system of landholding and removed the aristocratic warlords. Weights, measures and currencies were standardized throughout the land, and even such details as the width of chariot axles were regulated to help prevent ruts in the thousands of miles of new roads that were being constructed. The various and confusing local scripts were eliminated and one standardized script used throughout the land where a uniform and enormously detailed code of law was imposed everywhere.

Meanwhile hundreds of thousands of labourers and convicts were conscripted into Shihuang's great building projects – the canals and irrigation works plus the hundreds of palaces and pavilions for the nobles whom he had moved away from their own conquered territories in order to weaken their power. His most magnificent works, those which would make his name immortal, were also being carried out during this period of enormous change – the Great Wall, his fabled palace at Afang and his enormous tomb where his childless concubines were buried with him.

And in the year 213 B.C. an event took place which would make the First Emperor infamous to all succeeding generations – the burning of the country's books followed by the deaths of 460 scholars of the period whom he had buried alive.

From its original position in northwest China, the state of Qin became a vast empire.

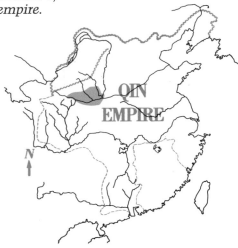

QIN EMPIRE

N

An early etching of the Great Wall.

Chronologies

General

c. 1765-1027 B.C.	Shang Dynasty
1027-256 B.C.	Zhou Dynasty
1027-771 B.C.	Western Zhou period
770-256 B.C.	Eastern Zhou period
770-481 B.C.	Spring and Autumn period
481-221 B.C.	Warring States period
221-207/206 B.C.	Qin Dynasty
206/202 B.C.-A.D. 220	Han Dynasty
206/202 B.C.-A.D. 9	Former Han period
A.D. 24-220	Later Han period

c. 300 B.C.	The Qin people build a long wall to resist the nomads of the north-west.
285 B.C.	Threatened rebellion in the state of Shu leads to the incorporation of the territory in the state of Qin.
c. 280 B.C.	Li Si, the future Grand Councillor to the First Emperor of China, is born in Chu state.
c. 261 B.C.	In Handan, Lu Buwei befriends Zizhu, the hostage prince of Qin and father of the First Emperor.
260 B.C.	The battle of Chang Ping is fought in which Qin slaughters 400,000 Zhao prisoners.
c. 258 B.C.	Zheng, the future First Emperor, is born.
c. 257 B.C.	Qin builds a bridge across the Yellow River.
256 B.C.	The troops of Qin depose the Zhou ruler.
251 B.C.	King Xiaowen summons Prince Zizhu and Lu Buwei to the capital of Xianyang.
250 B.C.	Prince Zizhu assumes the throne of Qin as King Zhuangxiang and Lu Buwei is appointed as Grand Councillor.
248 B.C.	Liu Bang, the future first Han emperor Gaozu is born.
247 B.C.	King Zhuangxiang dies. Li Si leaves Xunzi for Qin.
246 B.C.	Zheng, the future First Emperor, Qin Shihuang, ascends the Qin throne at the age of thirteen and his 'second father' Lu Buwei acts as regent. King Zheng makes Li Si a senior scribe. The Zhengguo canal opens
238 B.C.	Lao Ai rebels.
237 B.C.	Lu Buwei is exiled to the state of Shu where, two years later, he commits suicide. Li Si, along with other aliens, is saved from deportation.
237-219 B.C.	Li Si becomes justice minister.
233 B.C.	Han Feizi dies in Xianyang.
230 B.C.	Qin annexes the state of Han.
228 B.C.	Qin annexes the state of Zhao.
227 B.C.	Jing Ke tries unsuccessfully to assassinate King Zheng.
225 B.C.	Qin annexes the state of Wei.
223 B.C.	The state of Chu is subdued by

	General Wang Jian, and Qin then annexes it.
222 B.C.	Qin annexes the state of Yan.
221 B.C.	The last feudal state, Qi, is annexed by Qin. King Zheng becomes Emperor under the title of Qin Shihuang to mark the event.
	Li Si recommends that feudalism be abolished.
	Qin Shihuang establishes a uniform code of law, standardizes currency, measures, weights, and the written language, and founds a centralized state governed by a non-hereditary bureaucracy.
	The Qin empire is divided into thirty-six, later forty-two, commanderies connected by a network of roads.
	Weapons are collected, melted down and cast into statues at Xianyang.
	The influence of Taoism on Qin Shihuang becomes apparent.
	The tomb at Mount Li is mentioned for the first time.
219 B.C.	Qin Shihuang tours his empire.
	He tries unsuccessfully to obtain the elixir of immortality.
	The assassination attempt by Gao Jianli fails.
218 B.C.	Zhang Liang tries unsuccessfully to assassinate the First Emperor while he is on tour.
215 B.C.	Qin Shihuang commissions a second search for the elixir of immortality.
	General Meng Tian is victorious over the nomads.
214 B.C.	General Meng Tian is mentioned in connection with the construction of the Great Wall, which was accomplished over many years.
213 B.C.	Li Si advises the First Emperor to burn the country's books.
212 B.C.	Qin Shihuang buries 460 scholars at Xianyang and banishes Prince Fu Su, his eldest son, to the Great Wall.
	Construction is begun on the Afang palace.
210 B.C.	Nanhai is annexed.
	Qin Shihuang dies while on a tour of inspection.

	Zhao Gao and Li Si force Fu Su and Meng Tian to commit suicide; they bring back the body of Qin Shihuang to the capital, and announce the funeral and the accession of the younger son, Hu Hai, to the throne.
209 B.C.	The Second Emperor purges the imperial family, the court and the imperial bureaucracy. Zhao Gao influences the emperor. Chen She and Wu Gang, the first peasant leaders in Chinese history, rebel.
208 B.C.	Zhang Han successfully quells the rebellion but further uprisings soon engulf him.
	In the battle of Dingtao, Xiang Liang, a southern rebel leader, falls.
	Zhao Gao gains power at Xianyang.
	Li Si is executed.
207 B.C.	Zhang Han joins the rebel army.
	Nearly 200,000 soldiers are killed in the Xin'an massacre.
	Two weeks after presenting the young emperor with a stag, Zhao Gao compels him to commit suicide.
	Zi Ying, the nephew of the Second Emperor, ascends the throne.
	Zhao Gao dies.
	Liu Bang gains control of the Wei River valley through the battle of Lantian.
206 B.C.	King Zi Ying submits to Liu Bang.
	Under the leadership of Xiang Yu, rebel troops destroy Xianyang and the tomb of the First Emperor.
	Liu Bang seizes the Land within the Passes after a division of the empire by the rebels.
205 B.C.	Near Pengcheng, Xiang Yu defeats Liu Bang.
202 B.C.	Xiang Yu dies.
	Lui Bang is enthroned as Emperor Gaozu of the Han dynasty.
	'A general amnesty for the world' is proclaimed.
200 B.C.	Across the Wei River from Xianyang, Chang'an is made the Han capital.
90 B.C.	Death of Sima Qian, the historian and author of the *Shiji*.

The Heart of a Tiger

IT IS LARGELY FROM A SINGLE SOURCE, the *Records of the Historian* or *Shiji* by Sima Qian that we learn anything about the life of Qin Shihuang. Designed to cover the whole of human history, at least as the Chinese saw it, from its origins all the way down to the author's death in 90 B.C., the *Shiji* is China's first real work of history. Because of

*S*ima Qian, historian and author of the Shiji.

Sima Qian, the author of the *Shiji*, held the high official post of Grand Historian of the Han dynasty from 107 B.C., and began to write the official *Shiji* history three years later.

To prepare for his task, he consulted the records of his father, combed the Imperial library for documentary fragments and travelled widely to check private libraries and record the recollections of the learned and elderly.

For the next eight years, he combined his writing with other court duties, but in 99 B.C., he made the mistake of defending a certain general who had been forced to surrender to the Huns.

The autocratic emperor, Han Wudi, had him castrated and imprisoned for three years, but despite his suffering, Sima Qian continued his work in prison and when he was released at the age of fifty, became a palace secretary and completed his work in 91 B.C.

The *Shiji* is divided into 130 chapters and contains about 500,000 Chinese characters. It is still considered today, the definitive source of early Chinese history.

its antiquity, it has enjoyed immense prestige and almost universal admiration right up to the present day. Dealing with the state of Qin, both before and after unification in two chapters of "annals", it also provides additional information about prominent figures of the period in other biographical sections of the book.

However, even though the *Shiji* must rank as our most important evidence for the life and deeds of Qin Shihuang, its words must be treated with caution, for it was written a full century after the fall of the Qin dynasty. What sources still remained to the author we have no idea and there is a possibility that imagination could have taken the place of actual facts. The book was also written when Confucianism was the official state ideology and the philosophy of Legalism which had been dominant in Shihuang's time stood discredited. Although we do not know which philosophy the author of the *Shiji* held dear, it is obvious that Sima Qian was no admirer of the First Emperor. Later commentators on the *Shiji* were even more critical than he had been of Shihuang's dynasty and all it stood for, and there is good evidence that some of them inserted unflattering passages about the First Emperor. The problem of bias against Shihuang remains, therefore, a very real one.

There is a second barrier which also stands between us and our attempt to learn more about the real nature of the man who had made himself the country's August Emperor and it involves the nature of Chinese traditional historiography. Chinese history, for instance, is primarily court history written with a didatic purpose to serve as a "mirror" for future rulers and their ministers. Affairs which have no direct bearing on current events are left unrecorded and so, for instance, the first thirteen years of Shihuang's life, the period before he came to the throne, are a total blank. Even after he became the ruler, intimate details about his personal life are not recorded so that although we do know he had more than twenty children, we have no idea which of his many concubines were their mothers.

We do not even know if Shihuang ever had a favourite among his hundreds of women or ever raised one to the official position of empress. This is especially curious considering that Chinese historians from the Qin dynasty onwards, have recorded at least the names of all subsequent empresses of China. Although in Chinese legends, Shihuang has a reputation as a formidable lover endowed with enormous sexual prowess, a man who spread his amorous favours among the great number of beautiful women brought to his court from all over China, the truth about this side of his life may never be discovered.

A *reproduction of an 1881 edition of the* Shiji.

The Heart of a Tiger ...

There is a final problem facing any biographer of a Chinese ruler. The "annals" are short and cryptic, tending to deal with the *faits accomplis* of state policy and ignoring the part played in their formation by the ruler. This is of particular significance in the case of Qin Shihuang, since *China's First Unifier* by Professor D. Bodde, the standard academic treatment of Shihuang and his reign, attributes most of his achievements to the inspiration of his trusted advisor, Li Si.

There is no denying Li Si's importance, but the fact of the matter is that it was Shihuang who made the final decisions. It was also he who inspired court debates and decided which policies would be discussed, just as it was he who rewarded good advice and punished those who had misdirected him. In the final analysis, the Qin dynasty and its achievements were primarily the creation of one man – Qin Shihuang, the Son of Heaven, First Emperor of China.

In spite of these drawbacks, the *Shiji* does offer generally reliable information presented in a lively and anecdotal fashion. From it we draw our fullest physical description of Shihuang by one of his advisors, Wei Liao, who had been brought to the First Emperor's court and treated so generously that his ruler even shared his clothes, food and drink with him.

Wei Liao said:

The king of Qin (i.e. Shihuang) has the proboscis of a hornet and large (all-seeing) eyes. His chest is like that of a bird of prey and his voice like that of a jackal. He is merciless, with the heart of a tiger or a wolf. When he is in trouble, he finds it easy to humble himself, but when he is enjoying success, he finds it just as easy to devour human beings ... Should he achieve his goal of conquering the Empire, we shall all become his slaves. I cannot long cast in my lot with him.

After voicing this opinion, Wei Liao, who had been a competent advisor to Shihuang, prepared to flee from the state of Qin. Although aware of his criticism, Shihuang not only forced him to remain but gave him command of his armies. From this fascinating account we see that Shihuang was not only able to hear criticism directed towards him but clever enough to reward the critic in order to keep in his court a man whom he recognized to possess genuine talent.

Han Wudi, the emperor who was responsible for the castration of Sima Qian, the author of the Shiji.

There are many colourful tales surrounding Qin Shihuang's suspicious nature, and one of the more unusual legends tells of a special bronze mirror in his possession. This mirror, which was roughly four feet by six feet in size, projected inverted images of anyone who stood before it. It also had magical powers and could reveal the viscera and other internal parts of both men and women. It was useful in medical examinations and in unmasking any dangerous thoughts held by those in the presence of the Emperor. Thus even Qin Shihuang's own concubines could not hide their innermost thoughts from him.

Mirrors, such as the one pictured here, were made of a bronze containing a high percentage of tin. One side is quite decorative, while the reverse is smooth and polished to a high gloss.

Shihuang's Personality

FROM THE ACTIONS AND SPEECHES of the First Emperor recorded in the *Shiji* it is obvious that Shihuang was a man with a complex personality. As he grew older, like all of us, certain aspects of his character intensified while others became weaker. What had once been justifiable pride turned into megalomania, firmness into cruelty and a calm and rational approach toward the religious beliefs of his times became a frenzied and superstitious search for sacred herbs which would ensure his immortality.

The very first actions recorded in Shihuang's biography are those which occurred in the year 238 B.C. when he attained his majority, and took personal control of the government of the state of Qin. Learning of a plot against him which involved some of his most trusted ministers, he moved swiftly and decisively to suppress it. The principal plotters were dismembered, and their rotting skulls exposed on huge poles as a warning to others. The minor offenders, retainers and families of the guilty parties, were conscripted into forced labour or exiled to the unhealthy regions of the remote southwest. Decisiveness and ruthlessness were, therefore, the first of his characteristics to be revealed, and the fact that his reign began with a betrayal by his own mother and chief advisor perhaps instilled in him a sense of caution which in the last years of his life turned to paranoia, and an abject fear of death.

In that same first year of his reign, two other events indicated another strong facet of Shihuang's personality: the willingness to weigh advice and to reconsider his decisions. Although he had exiled his mother, who had been involved in the plot against him, he brought her back to the capital when he was warned that he would be seen as an unfilial son and that other states would oppose his action.

Shihuang had also issued an order for the expulsion of all aliens, because many of the conspirators against him were natives of other states who had come to Qin to throw in their lot with its rising power. He was persuaded to rescind the order by his advisor Li Si, who reminded his master that he possessed many valuable objects which came from outside his own state – pearls and jewels, horses and swords, beautiful women for his harem, and even drums made from the hide of the "divine crocodile." The alien politicians, Li Si said, were surely as valuable as these objects! And besides, if the emperor were to expel them, they would take their abilities to other states, and so strengthen his enemies.

Shihuang accepted this wise counsel, although it should be noted that Li Si had been astute enough to also appeal to Shihuang's vanity, praising his abilities, and reminding him of his desire to defeat the other Warring States and unify the land.

Qin Shihuang was a man with a deep interest in the sacred and a profound reverence for the supernatural. Studies of his life by Western historians too often use the term "superstitious" to describe him. This is wrong. He lived in a world populated by spirits and ghosts, and in a world in which the connection between Heaven and Earth was perceived to be much closer than is the case today. He sought to live a long time, perhaps forever, and those around him promised that he could achieve immortality. There were secrets hidden on the "Eastern Isles," and there were ways of synthesizing a pill or an elixir which could prolong life forever. Cinnabar was an important ingredient of these formulae and so were such other substances as mercury and phosphorous. Shihuang probably ingested all these substances, and rather than lengthening his life, they shortened it.

The search for immortality was a central theme in Qin Shihuang's life. In this painting entitled "The Festival of the Peaches of Longevity," various gods and goddesses have arrived at the home of the immortals to celebrate the gathering of the peaches of longevity which have taken 3,000 years to ripen.

The Visionary

THE NEXT ENTRIES in the *Shiji* all concern the military campaigns Shihuang directed over the next few years. All were victorious and reveal him as a leader with a keen grasp of military strategy and a single-minded purpose which was not only the defeat of his enemies, but the ending of the constant warfare and division which had characterized the last five centuries. Not only was he, therefore, a man of vision, a man with a high-minded goal, but he was also the possessor of supreme self-confidence, a man who believed he could achieve that which neither his ancestors before him nor any other ruler of his time had been able to achieve.

His very first words after the unification of China were: "I raised my troops to punish the six evil kings, and by grace of ancestral virtue, all six have been punished as they deserved to be. Now at last, I have brought peace to the whole land." As there is no reason to doubt the sincerity of his words at this time, it is clear that Shihuang took pride in his success. But as time went on, and as he enjoyed success after success, his justifiable pride turned to a far less attractive emotion, one which bordered on megalomania.

As we continue to read his biography, other traits emerge that demonstrate the singularity of Shihuang's personality. He believed in the respect due to authority and in his new position as emperor, and was determined to raise higher than ever before, the dignity of the throne and the awe in which he was held. He was willing to pursue policies he believed beneficial, such as the great levies of conscripted labour to build the Great Wall, even though he knew they would be unpopular. Although his biography records no act of compassion towards his subjects, individually or collectively, as he travelled about the country, he erected monuments and inscriptions which reminded his Blackhaired people that he provided domestic peace, encouraged agriculture, appointed fair and conscientious officials, and "worked without rest, day and night," for the benefit of all. This part of the inscriptions was indeed true for each night he pored over thousands of reports and documents, weighing rather than counting them. Throughout his reign, he retained both his energy and his workaholic habits, along with his passion for order, conformity and precision. He also continued to remain decisive, and if he became less and less tolerant of criticism and even constructive advice, he never lost sight of his goals and continued to work toward them.

Ritual jades. The cylinder represents Earth and the disc, Heaven.

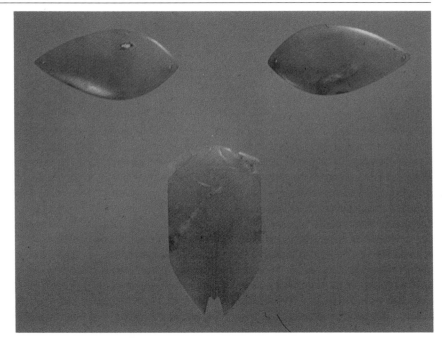

A *selection of jade pieces which were placed over the eyes and on the tongue of the deceased* *in order to prevent the decay of the body and the escape of the soul.*

Wealth and power in early China was displayed by the possession of jade and bronze vessels. Jade was especially important because of its religious significance.

The Chinese believed that man possessed twin souls that parted company at death – one to lie in a tomb and the other to ascend to the heavens. Both required the sacrifice and offerings of jade.

The kings of the Warring States valued jade more highly than gold and silver and sent armies of workers to faraway lands to bring back the stones. But jade was so hard, that metalsmiths had to carve it by using abrasive sand.

Several kings had jade strung into girdle pendants worn over their robes to make tinkling sounds when they walked through the palace and there are accounts of powdered jade being eaten in order to prolong life.

Although the historians of later ages tended to paint the First Emperor with broad brush-strokes, depicting him only in black and white, it is obvious that far more subtle colorations were needed to render a truer portrait of this complex and amazing ruler.

In the final analysis, the *Shiji* leaves us to come to our own conclusions about this complicated and enigmatic man.

The Origins of Shihuang

BECAUSE OF THE CHINESE veneration of antiquity, the leaders of the state of Qin, like the other rulers of the time, fashioned legends to make their origins date as far back as possible. Qin, therefore, claimed its people had originated in the third millenium B.C. when the granddaughter of a legendary figure ate the egg of a totemic swallow and gave birth to the line of Qin. More prosaic but reliable sources date the history of Qin back to 897 B.C. when the House of Zhou gave land to a tribal chieftain so he could breed horses. From its very beginnings, then, the horses of Qin and the horsemanship of its people were a part of the state's tradition and its cavalry would later make a great contribution to its military might.

A remarkable group of men, the ancestors of Shihuang, had been among the first of the 170-odd Zhou nobles to illegally raise their titles to the high rank of "Duke" (*gong*) and from 677 B.C. had advanced their capital eastward by stages until they had occupied most of the lands formerly owned by the Zhou. In 350 B.C. they finally came to rest in Xianyang which is only ten miles away from the present-day city of Xi'an.

Their advance had been carried out in the midst of large-scale warfare with their nomadic neighbours, the Rong, whom they eventually subdued. This constant battling with the warlike nomads had one very positive result for the state of Qin – it sharpened their warriors' military skills. However, the intermarriage with the Rong women that was the inevitable result of victory over the nomads had a negative aspect according to the more "civilized" states of the Central Plain who felt that the people of Qin had learned distressingly bad manners from their barbarian kinfolk.

Even Li Si, Shihuang's chief advisor, could not refrain from complaining about the barbaric music of the Qin to his master: *"Now the beating on earthen jugs, knocking on jars, plucking the strings of the guitar, and striking on thigh bones, all the while singing and crying 'Wu! Wu!' as a means of delighting the ear and eye: this indeed was the music of Qin."*

Although comparison between Shihuang's ancestors and the leaders of other states is difficult because Shihuang had these records destroyed later in his reign, it seems clear from the few sources that do still remain, that the state of Qin enjoyed a consistent succession of capable leaders.

Among the more noteworthy of Shihuang's remote ancestors was one Qin leader who was astute enough to provide protection to the disgraced leader of Zhou when he was forced to move his capital in the eighth century B.C. Another, Duke Mu (659-21 B.C.) was awarded the grand title of "Hegemon of the West" for his military successes against the barbarians.

Later there were other formidable leaders, especially after the Qin leaders decided that the title "Duke" was not sufficiently majestic and usurped the title of "King" (*wang*) in 325 B.C. One of these new Qin kings, Wu, surrounded himself with wrestlers and strongmen and astounded his peers with his physical strength until his attempt to lift an enormous bronze couldron over his head finally finished him off in 307 B.C. Then there was King Hui, a clever diplomat in his short reign, who used "beautiful women and comely boys" to subvert his enemies, and who formed, and then broke, a number of strategic alliances. Following him was King Zhaoxiang, an ambitious but careful ruler who summoned to his court the renowned advisors of his enemy rulers, and was

not ashamed to kneel (in private) before them. It was he who charted Qin's course through the crucial period when it was emerging as one of the seven paramount states. Perhaps he was able to manage this difficult task because he was in the habit of listening to his advisors, one of whom warned him that because Qin was becoming so powerful it would be "like a bone thrown among the hounds" to the other six states.

We can see, then, that Shihuang was heir to a tradition of strong, courageous leaders who were also clever statesmen. One of the more striking features possessed by the state of Qin was that its rulers were not only talented military leaders but brilliant strategists, as well. It was this combination of abilities that accounted for the state's rise. Later, Shihuang himself would show by his own actions, that he had studied and taken to heart the lessons in leadership displayed by his ancestors.

◁ *Horses were an important part of Shihuang's heritage as his ancestors were horse breeders.*

This bronze cauldron, called a ding, *is similar to the ritual vessel the Duke of Wu lifted above his head.*

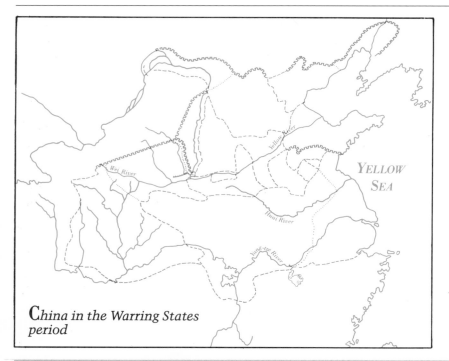

China in the Warring States period

A Product of the Warring States

THE PERIOD OF THE WARRING STATES of which the First Emperor was a product was a fluid, restless, brutal time, an era of fierce and unrelenting inter-state competition. The competing states vied with one another not just for supremacy but for actual survival, for all it took was one, single, fatal mistake for a state to be annexed by its more powerful neighbours. As the states became fewer and fewer, each one scrambled to adopt the newest techniques of agriculture, warfare, diplomacy and state organization – anything which would strengthen themselves and weaken or deter their neighbours. Men of ideas were eagerly sought after, and travelled freely from state-to-state, offering their advice or plans to the highest bidder. The intense competition resulted in astonishingly rapid technological progress, and by the time Shihuang had become emperor in 221 B.C., China probably exceeded the Mediterranean world in almost every measure of material civilization.

The darker side of this period was, however, an exceedingly

During the Warring States Period, warfare became more brutal, ravaging the peasants' lives and the land.

grim one. The Warring States Period (481-221 B.C.) produced a degree of bloodshed and misery which was to have few parallels throughout the remainder of Chinese history. The peasants' lives were wretched, as armies constantly marched across their fields, commandeering their meager crops, conscripting their sons and often raping their daughters. One scholar of the period has calculated that in the 241-year period between 463-222 B.C., there were only eighty-nine years which saw no major war.

And as time wore on, moving ever closer to Shihuang's birth-date of 259 B.C., the wars grew even more brutal and longer in duration. The number of troops engaged in each campaign reached figures that stagger the imagination. The state of Qin engaged in fifteen major campaigns between 364-234 B.C., and the number of casualties among enemy states alone is placed by the *Shiji* at almost 1.5 million! As the population of China at that time was about 40 million, it can be seen that the devastation was terrible and the loss of life staggering.

With the cost of war so great, it would be surprising if alternatives were not sought, and they were.

The diplomatic manoeuvering among the seven major states at the time of Shihuang's birth seems similar to our own century. There were alliances, north-south versus east-west, the "horizontal" versus the "vertical". Sometimes, two or three states allied against one, and betrayals were frequent, as today's ally became tomorrow's enemy. Diplomats travelled from state to state, announcing deterrent capabilities, offering bribes and convening disarmament conferences. Spies were everywhere and women were turned into pawns, used at the highest levels for strategic marriage alliances, and at the lowest, as "gifts" trained in all the seductive arts in order to subvert and distract rival rulers. Hostages of royal or noble birth were lodged as guarantees of good faith with enemy states, and it was out of this hostage system, that Shihuang was born.

Shihuang's Parents

THE STORY IS TOLD in the *Shiji* that Shihuang was the son of a merchant, a man called Lu Buwei, said to be an immensely rich dealer in luxury goods who "bought cheap and sold dear." At that time he was residing in the state of Zhao, Qin's foremost enemy, where the king of Qin had sent one of his younger sons, Zizhu, as a hostage.

Buwei was a shrewd and ambitious man, and realizing that the state of Qin was the rising power, and that the young prince, Zizhu, was living in straitened circumstances, he gained the young man's friendship by a gift of a thousand gold pieces, regarding it as "a sound investment in rare merchandise." Then he travelled to the state of Qin, determined to influence a change in the royal succession there.

Circumstances favoured him, for as luck would have it, the favourite wife of the king was childless. Showering her with gifts of jewels and jade and reminding her subtly, that as her beauty faded she was likely to lose her husband's favour, he persuaded her to use her charms on her husband and convince him to make his protegé, Zizhu, successor to the throne of Qin. When he became king, said Buwei, her future would then be secured as queen-mother. As Buwei had also freely dispensed his treasures and money to the couriers surrounding the king of Qin, it was not too difficult for the king's wife to get them to back her suggestion to the ruler who finally agreed. An elated Buwei rushed back to Zhao to convey the good news to Zizhu.

Now secure in his position as Crown Prince, Zizhu demanded even more favours from the wealthy merchant, promising to repay him when he became king. To Buwei's mortification, among the gifts the young prince demanded was the merchant's favourite concubine, a woman called Zhao Ji, the daughter of a wealthy family, who was also a skilled dancer, a seductive beauty, and judging from her later conduct, a woman of wanton tastes. Buwei reluctantly agreed to give her up, but unbeknownst to the young prince, she was pregnant by Buwei at the time.

When Prince Zizhu returned to the court of Qin, Zhao Ji accompanied him and gave birth to the squalling infant Zizhu believed to be his own son.

Zizhu ascended the throne of Qin in 249 B.C., and he immediately made Lu Buwei his Chancellor of State. When he died after a short reign of only three years, the son of Zhao Ji and Buwei succeeded him.

The *Shiji* thus informs us that Qin Shihuang was the bastard son of a merchant, a profession considered contemptible at that time, and a woman of easy virtue. Recent scholarship has been a little reluctant to accept this story, attributing it to bias against Shihuang and to later textual interpolation, but the fact remains that the story has been accepted as truth for more than 2,000 years and is believed by most Chinese today.

Qin Shihuang's mother, Zhao Ji.

Shihuang's mother had been the concubine of Lu Buwei, and according to the *Shiji*, she had also been the "finest dancer and the most seductive courtesan" in her native city of Handan in the state of Zhao. At the time of Shihuang, concubinage was common in the upper ranks of society. Its purpose was to ensure the birth of a male heir and, of course, in that firmly patriarchical society, to provide the male with an additional sexual outlet.

The law guaranteed certain rights to an officially-recognized concubine.

A courtesan, on the other hand, was a woman trained to please men. Unless she was employed in a tea-house or other such establishment, she worked independently, selling not so much her sexual favours, as her skills in dancing, singing and other arts like poetry. "Courtesans" were often the best educated women in Chinese society.

This painting shows Yang Guifei, a concubine of the "Brilliant Emperor" Minghuang in the 8th century. The Chinese regard her as the most beautiful woman in their history.

The Downfall of Lu Buwei

AS SHIHUANG WAS ONLY THIRTEEN when he came to the throne, the affairs of state were left in the hands of his Chancellor, Buwei, who soon became immensely rich and powerful, with "as many as ten thousand household retainers." Ashamed of his merchant origins, he surrounded himself with scholars and had them produce an encyclopedia to encompass all human knowledge. He then placed this book, which we still possess today, in the marketplace of the capital, offering a reward of a thousand gold pieces to any scholar who "could add or subtract a single word!" He also resumed his sexual relationship with his former concubine, now the queen mother, a move which would eventually lead to his downfall.

As Shihuang grew to manhood, Buwei became more and more nervous about his relationship with Shihuang's mother, and fearful that the young king would learn about their sexual liason. In order to disengage himself from the lascivious Zhao Ji, he conceived a bold plan. One of his retainers, a man by the name of Lao Ai, was famed for his enormous sexual endowment. The *Shiji* tells us that "in order to inflame" the queen-mother, Buwei had this man parade around with a cart-wheel balanced on his phallus! Hearing of this, Zhao Ji decided she wanted him as her lover and to prevent scandal, Lao Ai's beard and eyebrows were plucked to disguise him as a eunuch, and he was given to her. He must have lived up to her expectations for she made her new lover rich and powerful. In return, he gave her two sons, whom she concealed. Buwei's involvement in the affair apparently remained undetected, for not only did Shihuang continue to entrust to him the affairs of

The reputed father of Shihuang, Lu Buwei.

state, but he also bestowed on him the affectionate, honorary title of "Second Father."

But in 238 B.C. when Shihuang attained his majority and took the government into his own hands, ambitious informers soon revealed to him the scandal concerning his mother and her lover. Lao Ai, with the help of the queen-mother and perhaps Buwei, rose in rebellion, but Shihuang swiftly and ruthlessly suppressed the plot, and when Lao Ai escaped capture in the ensuing battle, Shihuang placed a price on his head – one million cash if he were taken alive, and half that sum if his head were presented to him! What terrible vengeance was Shihuang planning had Lao Ai been taken alive? Fortunately for him he was killed while in flight.

Shihuang, however, did get the opportunity to show what kind of punishment he would mete out to future plotters against his throne – other members of the rebellion, some of whom had held office within his palace, were dismembered and their bodies were exposed to the populace.

Although Buwei had been implicated in the affair, he was temporarily spared by Shihuang, but the queen-mother was sent into exile. Later he brought her back to the capital on the advice of his counsellors and installed her in her own palace where she quietly resided for the next seventeen years.

As for Lu Buwei, the following year he received a letter from Shihuang. "What have you done to benefit Qin?" the letter asked. Buwei took the hint, and the man whom historians consider to be the real father of the First Emperor killed himself by drinking poison.

In this punishment scene from an 18th-century European volume on Chinese history and culture, a criminal faces the magistrates who read out his crime and punishment.

Helman, Sculp.

Shihuang's Brilliant Minister – Li Si

IT WAS THE FALL of Lu Buwei that brought about the rise of Li Si, the man who, next to Shihuang himself, was destined to have the 'greatest influence on the political life of his times.

Li Si was a southerner, a petty clerk from the state of Chu, and we are told that one day, as he entered his office privy, he noticed that the rats there were scrawny, filthy and frightened. In the granary near his office, however, the rats were sleek, well-fed and arrogant. "A man's ability or lack of ability," he sighed, "is just like that of these rats. His condition in life depends on where he places himself." Soon realizing that Qin was emerging as the strongest of the states, he travelled there in 247 B.C., the year before the thirteen-year-old Shihuang succeeded to the throne. Determined to place himself amongst the powerful men of the time, he entered the service of Lu Buwei.

Ambitious and opportunistic, Li Si soon contrived to meet the young king of Qin, and by adroit flattery and clever advice not only won Shihuang's confidence, but was also given the title of Alien Minister, an honour sometimes conferred in Qin upon advisors from other states. He engaged in secret diplomacy, manipulating a network of agents and spies, and found time to continue the studies he had earlier begun under the great Confucian philosopher, Xun Zi.

His career was almost cut short in 237 B.C. when Shihuang, disgusted with the rebellious activities of Lao Ai, Lu Buwei, and other alien politicians who had come to Qin, issued a decree for the expulsion of all aliens. Li Si, in a smooth and carefully-worded speech, persuaded him to cancel his order, and as a reward was promoted to Minister of Justice.

We hear no more of him until the conquest was complete, but presumably he was at Shihuang's side, offering advice from his own experiences in espionage, and in 221 B.C. when the Qin dynasty was proclaimed, he became Grand Councillor. From that time until the death of the First Emperor, he was the most powerful of state ministers, although he never did achieve dominance over Shihuang who always made sure that the final decisions during his rule would be his alone.

However, many of Shihuang's policies are attributed to Li Si. He stood firm against majority opinion in 221 B.C. when the Emperor was advised to restore the feudal system of nobles, and hence played a role in Shihuang's centralization of China.

To Li Si is also attributed the systematization of the variant scripts of the time and the composition of China's first dic-

tionary. He accompanied Shihuang on all of his tours of inspection and is said to have been the author of some of the great stone inscriptions left behind to praise his master's achievements. But he is remembered, above all, as the man who advised Shihuang to decree the "Burning of the Books," and it is because of this act, that he shares in the hatred with which historians have regarded Shihuang.

His power remained undiminished until the end of his life. His sons and daughters were married into the Emperor's family, and so great was his influence, that the *Shiji* remarks, "the number of chariots and horsemen [begging favours] at his front gate, could be numbered in the thousands."

A faithful servant of Shihuang until the very end, Li Si was with the First Emperor when he died on his last tour which he had taken in order to search for the elixir of immortality. It was Li Si who was instrumental in placing on the throne, Prince Hu Hai, by tricking Shihuang's actual heir-apparent into killing himself. Ironically, it was because the Second Emperor believed that Li Si was showing disloyalty to him by not properly completing the tasks set out by his father Shihuang, that Li Si was sent to prison where he suffered the Five Tortures: the slitting of the nose; amputation of a hand; amputation of a foot; castration, and finally, execution.

L i Si was put to death by the Second Emperor of Qin after trying time and again to warn him of the result of his follies. In prison, he is said to have exclaimed, *"The Second Emperor has attacked his elder and younger brothers, without examining their guilt, and has executed his loyal ministers, one by one without looking at their misfortunes. He has undertaken great constructions of palaces and has heavily taxed the whole world, without considering the consequences... We shall soon see rebels taking the city of Xianyang and deer wandering through the palace courtyards."* Experienced statesman that he was, his words were prophetic.

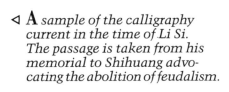

◁ **A** *sample of the calligraphy current in the time of Li Si. The passage is taken from his memorial to Shihuang advocating the abolition of feudalism.*

L*i Si, the most important of Shihuang's ministers.*

An Assassination Attempt

IN THE YEAR 227 B.C., after twenty years of successful warfare and with his troops only six years away from total victory, Shihuang almost lost his life.

This famous event, often depicted in Chinese art, fiction and drama, was the first of three assassination attempts which Shihuang would survive, and it was the most serious. Had it been successful, it would have changed the course of Chinese history.

The would-be killer, Jing Ke, was a man from the northeastern state of Yan, a state exhausted by defeat and terrified that it would soon become the next of Qin's victims. A clever man, and a sensualist, fond of wine and women, he was also an expert in the martial arts and deadly with his sword. He had befriended a renegade general from Qin, and when his prince suggested to him that the assassination of Shihuang was the only way to stop the Qin advance, he went to his friend for advice. The general laughed, knowing that Shihuang was a suspicious man and that no citizen of Qin, much less a foreigner, ever got past his guards without a thorough search. He advised Jing Ke that the only way to gain audience was to offer Shihuang something he really wanted, and here, said the general, he could help. Shihuang wanted his head, and had offered a great reward for it. Why not take it? Jing Ke hesitated, but the general immediately slit his own throat and rather than let the head go to waste, Jing Ke sealed it in a box and set off for Qin.

He also carried with him maps of of the terrain of his state, a closely-guarded secret in those days because of their use to an invading army. Within these maps, he concealed his famous dagger, razor-sharp and tipped with a poison so deadly that "when it drew so much as a thread of blood," the victim died instantly.

Jing Ke's gifts secured him an audience with the king, and he was allowed to mount the dias where Shihuang stood alone and unprotected. Unrolling his maps, he seized the hidden dagger in one hand and Shihuang's sleeve in the other. Startled though he was, Shihuang was too fast for the assassin. He tore away his sleeve and took shelter behind a stone pillar, trying to draw his own sword as Jing Ke hurled the deadly blade. Missing Shihuang by inches, it lodged in the pillar, and Shihuang, it is said, fainted dead away.

After Shihuang's guards had seized Jing Ke, he was immediately beheaded and his corpse mutilated, while Shihuang vented his fury by launching a full-scale attack on Yan. His generals inflicted terrible casualties, annexed much territory, and brought back to Shihuang the head of the ruler who had ordered the assassination. Five years later, the state of Yan fell.

In this Han representation of the assassination attempt, Qin Shihuang is holding an imperial jade disc while Jing Ke is seized by Shihuang's physician. The dagger was so sharp it could even pierce the stone pillar.

From that time onward, Shihuang took ever-greater precautions to ensure his own safety. And he became less trusting of those around him. Near the end of his life this distrust had turned into a paranoia so severe that he had the roads leading to his hundreds of palaces covered over so that he could not be seen.

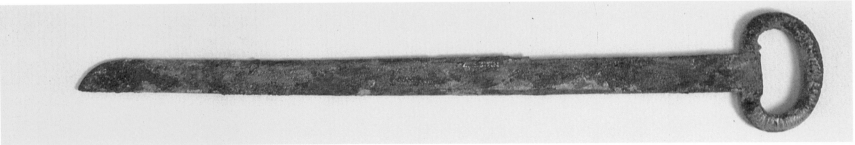

Jing Ke is said to have purchased the sharpest dagger in the empire for 100 gold pieces and had it dipped in deadly poison by an artisan for his mission to assassinate the First Emperor.

戦争

THE LAND OF HUNGRY GHOSTS

Warfare in
Ancient China

The Manners of Barbarians

THE HOUSE OF ZHOU, which had come to power in about 1027 B.C., was responsible for a system of feudalism in which the lands were parcelled out to members of their royal family. Eventually these nobles became more and more independent and broke off into separate principalities and then states. In 771 B.C., when nomad barbarians sacked Zhou's capital, the royal house was forced to move to a site near the present-day city of Luoyang.

Although Zhou continued to reign, it no longer ruled the country. Its control was no longer based on its military might but rested merely on its people's reverence for the awesome rituals it performed such as the annual sacrifice to Heaven. Gradually, however, its influence further waned, and in 256 B.C. the House of Zhou became extinct when it was snuffed out by the State of Qin which had become a mighty military power.

The other states, which still retained a reverence for the Zhou heritage, were appalled at Qin's domination and one of their officers wrote to his leaders about the Qin state:

"Qin customs are those of the Rong and Di (barbarians). She has the heart of a tiger or a wolf ... and is ignorant of propriety, integrity and virtue."

Those, however, who had studied the history of the fierce state of Qin, were not in the least surprised by its bold action. Qin's rulers had usurped the title of "duke" and since 677 B.C. had advanced their capital eastward by stages until they had occupied most of the lands formerly possessed by the House of Zhou and had come to rest in 350 B.C. at Xianyang.

Although Qin's early history had been dominated by warfare with the nomad barbarians, the Rong, whose manners they had been accused of adopting, their occupation of the more civilized Zhou people had smoothed their rough edges. It had also given them greater political sophistication which their leaders had learned to put to very effective use.

The extent of the territory of the House of Zhou.

▷ One of the rulers of Zhou.

WARFARE

Shihuang's Philosophy of War

BY THE TIME QIN SHIHUANG had taken control of his government, the young man had been well-trained by his mentors in the sophisticated political traditions the Qin had learned from the clever statesmen of Zhou. One of the more striking facts he would have learned about the fierce dukes and kings who were his ancestors was that they saw their roles more as strategists than warriors and saw no need to lead their troops into battle.

Shihuang appeared to agree with their strategy, and despite the many conquests and bloody battles conducted by his troops, it is nowhere recorded that he was ever present on any battlefield. As brilliant a military tactician as his ancestors had been, he began to select his generals on the basis of merit rather than social status. And he believed in a certain philosophy of war:

"War is that matter which is most vital to the state. It is the province of life or death, and the path which leads to survival or to ruin." These are the opening words of Sun Zi's *Art of War*, China's classic manual of strategy and tactics.

Dating from somewhere between 400 and 320 B.C., it was a work widely distributed in the later days of the Warring States Period and must have been essential reading for Shihuang who gloried in his victories, savoured the fruits of revenge and – at least in the beginning – set his goal as peace for his Blackhaired people.

No matter how noble the aims, however, his wars added to the burden of the people who had been plagued by constant strife for a long, long time.

In the beginning there were Three Dynasties – Xia, Shang and Zhou – traditionally spanning the period from 2205 to 256 B.C. They, in turn, had followed from a much longer period of rule by sage-kings and culture heroes who had presided over a "Golden Age" and who are said to have passed the throne, not to the eldest son, but to the most virtuous of their subjects.

Only with "Yu the Great," the founder of Xia and the man who built the country's first dikes and canals, did primogeniture come to China. Yu's achievements were so popular that the lords around him insisted that his son succeed him. And so was founded the dynastic principle.

The Xia, still considered by many to be a legendary dynasty, were probably nothing more than the paramount tribe in a tribal period. When the Shang who succeeded them and are regarded by most historians to be a kingdom, they controlled their alliance of tribes by periodic hunts and a loose feudal relationship.

When the Zhou came to power, in about 1027 B.C., they refined and extended this rudimentary feudalism, establishing 1,773 fiefdoms which were to a large extent self-governing. The Zhou rulers called themselves "Sons of Heaven" and decreed that their lands encompassed "All under Heaven."

In reality, however, they could not control their vassals and this weakness was graphically demonstrated in 771 B.C. when the lords failed to respond to the ruler's beacon fires to defend the capital from the barbarian Rong. The result was total defeat of the Zhou and their flight to safer lands in the east where they set up a new capital.

At this time there were only 170 principalities. By the time Shihuang came to the throne of Qin in 246 B.C., this number had been lowered by bloody strife to only seven. These were the states of Qin, Zhao, Yan, Qi, Chu, Wei, and Han.

◁ *The legendary sage-king Yu the Great who, it is said, had taught the Chinese the techniques of irrigation and flood control 2,000 years before the birth of Qin Shihuang.*

The size of the armies as reported by the *Shiji* varied widely.

Shihuang in his unification campaigns is reported to have had an army of 600,000. The later Han dynasty, on the other hand, seemed to get by with an army ranging from 130,000 to 300,000 which included troops and cavalry.

Shihuang's huge force is believable, however, when it is noted that he mobilized 100,000 men to labor on the Great Wall and 700,000 to build his tomb.

Shang Yang's Reforms

Shang Yang, the early Qin statesman, whose reforms strengthened the state.

THE REDUCTION IN NUMBER of the feudal states can be traced to several factors, but the most important reason was war. The states in this period were rudimentary in organization and the ruler or duke usually presided from a walled city which he tried to defend against his avaricious rivals while at the same time trying to protect the surrounding peasantry who were his only source of revenue.

The peasants' lives were generally miserable. Subject to land taxes in most states from 594 B.C. and always liable for military conscription, they worked from dawn to dusk for a bare subsistence and were protected from marauders only by the mud walls of the villages they returned to at night.

The iron dukes, thus took much and gave little, unmercifully using the peasants to wage war in order to protect their lavish lifestyle at court.

Shihuang was among the first rulers to realize that, instead of war, agriculture was the essential occupation of the state and that if the peasants were treated properly the whole land might some day be unified.

His new policies arrived just in time because the states had been gradually destroying themselves and each other for years. The expansion of the states on the periphery of the Central Plain, due in part to their geographical advantages, had allowed them to gobble up the smaller principalities which lined the Yellow River.

The northern states, such as Zhao, for instance, had also used cavalry as a war instrument earlier and more successfully than their neighbours and it was here that trousers first became a part of the soldiers' uniforms, showing the growing importance of horsemanship in war.

Initially equal in power, the Warring States slowly exhausted themselves as they mounted ever more deadly experiments in warfare. In Qin, the reforms which made the state truly strong took place only about a century before Shihuang became king. As the other states exhausted themselves in battle, Qin's geographical position kept it aloof and it was not regarded as a great threat, at least in the beginning.

The architect of Qin's change was Shang Yang (390-338 B.C.), a man of some military reputation who answered the call to battle from Duke Xiao of Qin in 361 B.C. and whose advice helped the state to regain lands lost to their neighbours.

Also a man of great political acumen, Lord Shang transformed the face of Qin by dividing part of it into 31 counties, each administered by a centrally-appointed magistrate instead of a feudal lord. He also raised the status of the peasants, allowing them to buy and sell land, thus attracting new immigration from the surrounding states. Because of these policies, the population grew larger and provided more soldiers for Qin's army.

New laws also appeared, "sparing neither the powerful nor the high," and fierce punishments were meted out to criminals, such as boiling alive, dismembering at the waist and the rending apart of the body by chariots.

Systems of reward were also established and honorary ranks were lavishly bestowed for service to the state. Most were given for military valor: *"Whomever cuts off one enemy head will be awarded a single degree of rank."*

Thus Shang Yang's reforms succeeded in strengthening the state of Qin when China, as we know it today, was truly a land of "life or death."

As this ancient scroll shows, agriculture has always been central to the Chinese way of life.

Lord Shang Yang is important in the later unification efforts of Shihuang because he developed early laws and made attempts at standardization and currency changes. But Shang Yang nearly did not become the first minister of Qin.

The descendent of a concubine, Shang Yang was raised in the state of Wei and served under the prime minister who recognized his ability. When the prime minister became ill, the king visited him and the prime minister recommended Shang Yang as his successor.

"If you do not mean to take my advice and employ him," warned the dying prime minister, *"take my advice and have Yang killed. Do not let him leave the country."*

Alas, the king did not act and Shang Yang was eventually recruited by the Duke of Qin, later to become first minister there and lay the groundwork for Qin's eventual domination of all the states.

49

Warfare in the Spring and Autumn Period

CHINESE HISTORIANS DIVIDE this era into two parts. The first, taking its name from a book by Confucius, was called the Spring and Autumn Period and lasted from 770-481 B.C. The second, which ran to the Qin unification in 221 B.C., is called the Period of the Warring States.

It was a time of huge growth in the scope, frequency and brutality of war. In one 130-year period, the *Shiji* recorded 15 major battles or campaigns in which Qin was involved and the death toll – just for Qin's opponents – amounted to 1,489,000, a figure possibly exaggerated by Qin to impress the other states.

During the Spring and Autumn Period, battles were carefully conducted according to recognized codes, complete with chivalry and a good deal of ceremony. Actual combat involved far more propriety than savagery, and there are many documented episodes of archers courteously exchanging arrows with one another until one of them was finally killed.

In another case, while the Chu troops were observing the Yan army, one of their spies noticed that the Yan always favoured the left wing and told the officers that this fact surely indicated that the Yan king was sure to be on that side. Although the right flank of the Yan army was considered to be more vulnerable to attack, the Chu commander ordered his forces against the left, saying, "*If we do not oppose the king, we are no sort of opponent.*" The result was that the Chu army was soundly defeated, albeit nobly.

One of the other codes of battle at that period was the unwritten rule that one could never take advantage of an adversary in distress. There is recorded evidence that one battle was not rejoined because the enemy had not yet cleared up its dead. When the field was finally swept clear of bodies, their opponents who had been chivalrously waiting to begin the attack on them, moved their army forward only to discover that their good manners had been taken advantage of and the enemy had stolen away during the night.

The *Shiji* also speaks of the soldiers' boldness and resolution:

Confucius explaining the rising power of Qin to the dukes of other states.

When one takes up arms he must heed the code of war, which calls for them. To kill the enemy is resolute, and to display resolution in the highest degree is boldness.

If one does otherwise, he should be killed in disgrace.

Neither fear nor a sense of inferiority were permitted to affect performance in the carefully plotted campaigns.

One conflict was marked by this observation:

Fighting is a matter of valorous spirit. When the drum first beats, that excites the spirit. With a second beating, it is diminished. With a third, it is exhausted.

When theirs was exhausted, ours was abundant. Therefore we conquered them. Yet these great states are difficult to fathom, and I feared there might be an ambush. But I observed their chariot tracks were disorderly and when I looked at their banners, they were drooping.

Thereupon we pursued them.

Divination was considered so important that in the case of one fight, a general of Qin, worried about the outcome, summoned a music master who, as the *Shiji* records it, sang a song, and then reported to the general,

"It will do no harm. I have been loudly singing a northern melody and then again a southern one. The latter was not strong and had the tone of many deaths.

"The enemy will certainly accomplish nothing."

The blind musician thus fortified the Qin general and assured him he was in tune with the heavenly gods. It must have worked because the battle was short and decisive with Qin winning easily.

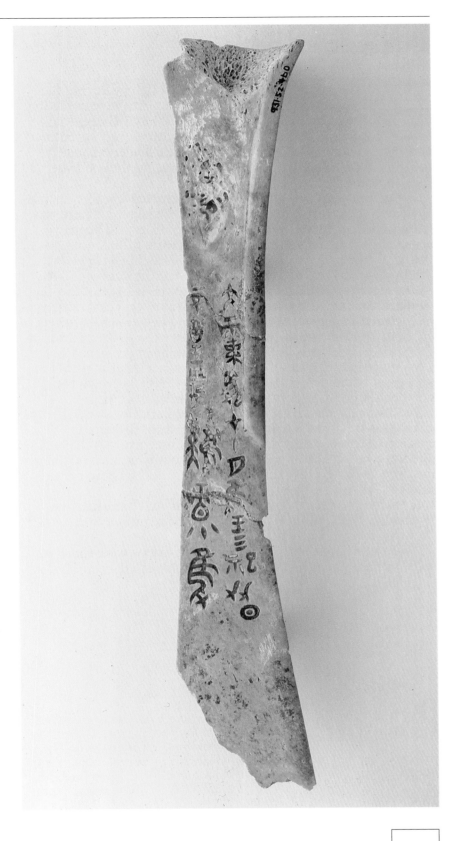

Oracle bones were used from at least 1500 B.C. for the purposes of divination. Characters were inscribed in the bones and diviners read the oracle from cracks which appeared when the bones were placed over fire. Some scholars speculate that skilled diviners could control the configuration of the cracks.

The Conduct of Battle

BATTLES WERE NOT ENGAGED IN lightly during the Spring and Autumn Period. The spirits were consulted through omens, dreams or professional diviners and if the signs were unfavourable the attack was sometimes aborted. It was also necessary for the state leaders to justify military action and to show that right was on their side before they moved into action.

If an army had been victorious, the defeated troops were pursued and, if captured, held for ransom or enslaved. There was little indiscriminate slaughter and if territory had been annexed, few of the vanquished nobles were killed, nor was the royal line ever extinguished. During the huge three-day feasts that followed victories, the blood of the dead was occasionally smeared on the war drums and the left ear of the dead soldiers and the surrendered captives was cut off and used as a tally to record the number of men killed and slaves acquired.

Many vivid accounts of actual battles exist in the records of the Spring and Autumn Period and have been preserved in a work called the *Zuozuan*. Among them is a lengthy report on a great battle which took place in 647 B.C. between the northern state of Jin and the southern state of Chu.

Each side divided its forces into three battalions and the war chariots were divided into two formations of fifteen each. The chariots were supported by 125 footsoldiers. Prior to the battle, one three-man chariot penetrated the enemy ranks, and one of the officers darted into the enemy ranks, daringly cut off a soldier's left ear and took him prisoner.

Returning to his own lines, this unknown charioteer also stopped to kill a stag and presented it to the pursuing enemy to show his coolness under fire.

When this battle actually started, the troops were manoeuvered by signals from flags and drums. The charioteers shot at the enemy with arrows and the footsoldiers fought with spears and swords. When the signal for retreat was mistakenly sounded by a Jin drummer and as the army retreated back across a river, a Jin officer promised a reward to the first men who made it back to shore. Soon the boats were full of the severed fingers of the Jin soldiers attempting frantically to climb into the departing boats.

Although battles in the period 770-481 B.C. were chivalrously conducted, they eventually became more and more brutal. In one 130-year period, the death toll for Qin's opponents amounted to 1,489,000.

The state of Jin was disgracefully defeated in the great battle, but the leader of the Chu refused to gloat over his enemies or, as was the custom after a victory, to bury the defeated dead in a great mound as a monument to the glory of the conquering army.

Instead, he made a remarkably idealistic speech about the preservation of the state, the need for harmony among the rival states and the bestowal of peace upon the peasants, the better to enlarge the general wealth.

Although a noble attempt by the Chu leader, his words had little lasting effect as the battles became even more frequent and savage as time went on.

During the Warring States Period, there were many famed tacticians, among them Tian Dan of Qi who once broke out of a siege by the forces of Yan when escape seemed impossible. The *Shiji* says:

"He assembled more than a thousand bulls, covered them in red silk, painted them in many colours so that they resembled dragons, lashed daggers to their horns, and to their tails he tied straw soaked in oil. At night the straw was set afire and the bulls were released through rifts in the city wall, followed by five thousand strong men. Driven mad by their burning tails, the bulls attacked the army of Yan, taking them by surprise. To the men of Yan, the bulls illuminated by the unearthly glow of their flaming tails, seemed like dragons bent on destruction. After the bulls came the five thousand men, mouths gagged, followed by the entire population of the city shouting and banging on copper vessels, the old and infirm beating so loudly that the noise shook heaven and earth. Yan's forces retreated in terror and confusion, pursued by the throng. Every city they passed threw off Yan's bondage and flocked to Tien Dan's support.

The Warring States Period

A S THE WARRING STATES PERIOD began in 481 B.C. the *Shiji* tells us that battles became longer, fiercer and were fought on a much larger scale. Brutality and cruelty became the norm and chivalry was increasingly disregarded. Wholesale slaughter of the conquered often followed a large-scale battle and according to the *Shiji*, 450,000 Zhao soldiers were massacred by the Qin army after a battle in 260 B.C.

There is evidence, however, that these figures were so high because they covered not only the dead and wounded but also the captives and deserters from the enemy ranks. But it is clear that no tactic was too vicious to use and, on more than one occasion, dikes were deliberately breached which not only drowned great numbers of the enemy but innocent civilians as well.

In the third century B.C., Qin, as well as its foes, conscripted boys as young as fifteen to fight and the size of the standing armies often reached a figure as high as 600,000.

◁ T*he lightning-fast footsoldiers and cavalry were decisive factors in Qin's victories over other states.*

T*he importance of war is demonstrated by the care and expense lavished on these fittings. The round bronze piece* served a decorative purpose while the others were attached to chariots to hold the crossbow.

The legendary war chariots of Qin were drawn by four horses and carried three men – a driver in the middle with the leader on the left and a spearman on the right.

The chariot directed the footsoldiers – anywhere from thirty to seventy-five men – with drums, gongs, and flags, so that the sounds of battle were deafening. Often the chariots were equipped with scythes on the axles and could cut a swath of blood through the ranks of the enemy.

Our best clues as to the type of weapons and the kinds of armour worn by the Qin soldiers in the Warring States Period come from the tomb of Shihuang, one of the most important archaeological finds of all time.

Here, in the 1970s, archaeologists discovered a vast buried army of terracotta warriors, archers, and footsoldiers each armed and set up in perfect formation for battle, along with their chariots. No two are alike and each warrior bears distinctive facial features. Three pits have now been unearthed showing the diversity of weapons and the sophistication of battle formations during Shihuang's time. Shihuang ordered these clay warriors created to protect his sacred mausoleum, a tomb that has still not been uncovered on the site at Mount Li near modern day Xi'an.

Shihuang's Buried Army

UNTIL A LITTLE OVER A DECADE ago, there was relatively little information available about warfare in the Qin period. Then, in the early 1970s, the situation changed dramatically with the discovery of a vast buried army of clay warriors, armed and in perfect formation for battle with archers, chariots, and footsoldiers. For the first time, information was available on armour, military formations, chariot construction, weaponry and even soldiers' hairstyles. Previous to this, the history of warfare in this period had been written from fragmentary records, but here, a whole army, in lifelike detail, had been perfectly preserved. Within a few years, not one but three pits had been discovered, each one containing artifacts which provided a more complete picture of Qin period warfare.

Because the Qin was involved in near-perpetual warfare with other states from the seventh to the third centuries B.C., it is hardly surprising to find quite a diversity among weapon types and a sophistication in military strategies and formations. Warfare took a prominent position in Qin society, and many of their developments in armaments, armour and tactics were to form the foundations for the military organization of successive decades.

Archaeologists have found many Qin period tombs containing a wide variety of artifacts, related to Qin culture, including lacquerware, ceramic and bronze vessels, and bronze weapons. Undoubtedly the best artifacts for studying warfare in the Qin, however, come from the three pits containing life-size terracotta warriors, set up and buried as part of the funerary trappings for Qin Shihuang. Each of the warriors in the buried army is individually modelled, and so detailed that historians are able to study the various types of armour worn by the soldiers to determine how they were constructed, what materials were used in their manufacture, and even how the warrior put it on. Although the warriors of the buried army are modelled from clay, their weapons are real, and from these we are able to gain valuable information both on the advancement of weaponry and on the metal-working technology used to create their swords, crossbows and other tools of war.

A *terracotta infantryman kneels in anticipation of battle.*

Mounted on a long pole, the dagger axe was a formidable weapon in the battles of Shihuang's time.

The head of one of the terracotta horses, complete with bronze bridle.

Failure on the battlefield was never tolerated as this telling of the Qin conquest of Yan demonstrates:

"The general said 'I'll just exterminate these fellows and then I'll have them for breakfast' and without armoring his horses he charged. He was wounded by an arrow and the blood ran down to his shoes, but he did not break off the sound of the drum.

"He said 'I am in pain' but his charioteer said: 'Sire, bear it.'

"The general then said: 'The ears and eyes of the army are upon our banner and drum. By those, they advance and retreat. While one man can still guide this chariot, we can yet gain the day. How can we, on account of pain, bring our lord's great affairs to failure?

"To don armor and take up arms is to court death. If the pain is not yet mortal, strive against it.' "

"With that, he drove his chariot onward and the army followed. This was the fierceness of the Qin."

Warriors

From the almost 8,000 figures unearthed in the three pits (a fourth pit was found to be empty), we can see that the pits were designed in military formations. It has even been suggested that the buried soldiers represent actual army units. Pit 1 is the largest, containing primarily infantrymen: unarmoured bowmen and crossbowmen, archers, armoured infantrymen and chariots with charioteers. Pit 2, smaller in size, contains a more complex layout of military personnel divided into four units of archers, chariots and cavalrymen. Pit 3 contains only sixty-eight figures, who may, by virtue of the small size of the group, represent officers or a command unit. Most of the soldiers wear long double-layer tunics which wrap in front and are belted at the waist; leggings; and square-toed footwear. A thick fabric roll is worn at the neck. This would offer protection against chafing at the neck for those wearing armour.

The hairstyles are elaborate. Each is fashioned individually, to such a fine degree that one can see every strand of hair. For the infantryman, the hair is pulled up on the top of the head and is tied in a chignon, slightly to the right. Some of the hairstyles also incorporate elaborate plaiting into the designs.

A number of the figures, most notably the cavalrymen, wear soft caps with chin straps. The officers and charioteers have crisp bonnets, and although those of the charioteers are not as fancy as those of the officers, the difference in the headwear styles may indicate a difference in rank between the charioteers and the capless regular infantry.

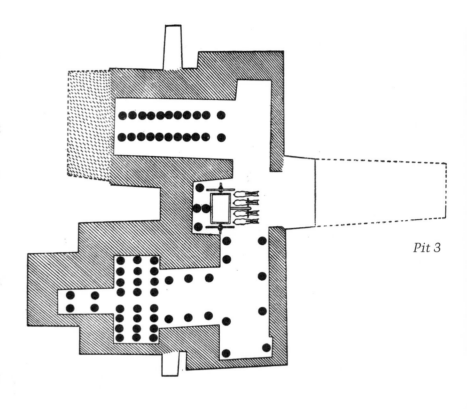

Pit 3

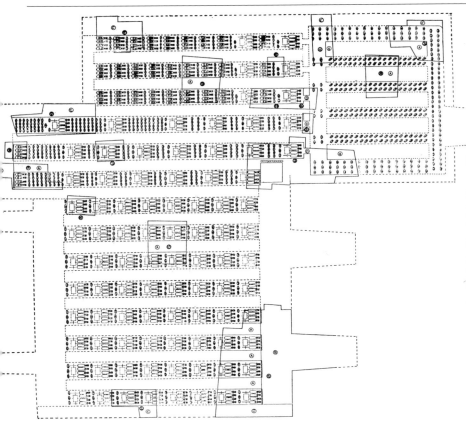

Pit 2

The arrangement of soldiers in Pit 1 is remarkably similar to this: the unarmoured bowmen and crossbowmen occupy the front ranks; behind them, eleven corridors of soldiers stand in formation. The two outer ranks contain two rows of archers, the outermost of which faces outward, prepared against any flank attacks. The other line faces ahead with the rest of the army. In the remaining nine columns, armed and armoured infantry stand at the ready. Within these ranks, not far behind the unarmoured infantry, are six chariots, each pulled by a team of four horses. A charioteer and a warrior man each chariot. Protecting the rear of this army of nearly 6,000 figures are three lines of armoured infantry.

In Pit 2, by comparison, the force is composed mainly of chariots and cavalry, whereas Pit 1 contains mostly infantry. Pit 3 has a large number of officers. Taken together, then, the three pits represent components of a single army in an arrangement common even to Western armies through the nineteenth century. The main body of the force is composed of infantry, while a smaller, more mobile force of mounted troops is detached to act separately, and a command unit oversees the whole operation.

Pit 1

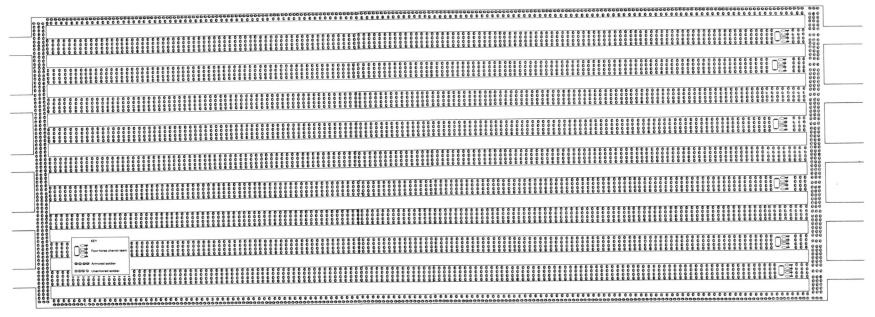

When buried, the figures were painted but much of this paint has since flaked off. The paint reflected different uniform colours which served to distinguish between various units of the army. At least two colour schemes are present in Pit 1. The first group had green robes with lavender collars and cuffs. Their trousers were dark blue, and their black shoes had red laces. The armour consisted of black plates, white rivets, purple cords and gold buttons. The second group had red tunics, with the collars and cuffs in pale blue. The armour was dark brown with red or light green rivets and orange cords. Brightly coloured, the massed troops would have presented an imposing sight when freshly painted and must have looked remarkably similar to a real army.

The organization of the buried army is precise and regular, with the soldiers organized in columns. Two military instruction manuals of the period suggested that military formations should be organized as follows:

long-range crossbows in front, halberds behind,
bows are the outer layer, halberds and shields the inner,
skilled soldiers and strong bows on the flanks.

A *terracotta general, wearing his decorated armour, stands tall.*

Armour

Armour used by early Chinese soldiers covered only part of the body. There was usually a breast plate, which could sometimes also have a section which covered the back as well. Pieces which protected the shoulders and upper arms were sometimes attached to this to form a shirt-like covering for the upper body. Helmets were occasionally used to protect the head.

Until the excavation of the pits, very little was known about Qin period armour. The first evidence of armour in China comes from tombs in Anyang which date to the Shang dynasty (c. 1765-1027 B.C.). This armour consisted of leather strips brightly painted in red, white, yellow and black. Nearly one thousand years later, during the Warring States Period (481-221 B.C.), leather plates, lacquered and laced together with leather thonging, were used to protect soldiers from enemy weapons. There is some evidence of armour being made of bronze, but this was only used in areas outside central China, and therefore was not relevant to the Qin.

Helmets made of bronze also date to the Shang dynasty, and while texts mention a helmet of iron, only one such piece of armour made of iron plates laced together has been found, and it dates to the fourth century B.C. For centuries, this leather armour provided enough protection against contemporary bronze weapons. Then, however, the change in weaponry in the late Warring States period was the catalyst for changes in body armour.

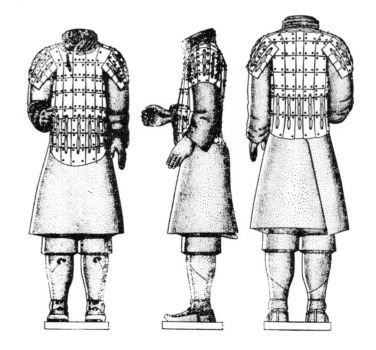

The pits give us the most complete and detailed information on Qin period armour. There are eight different styles which may be classified into two groups. In the first, leather forms the foundation layer to which rectangular scales were attached. For the second type, the scales are strung together without a base layer. The armour was slipped on over the head and buckled with a right front closure. It is difficult to know what this armour was made of, but scholars feel that it most likely was made of lacquered leather, as no metal plates of this size have been discovered.

Commanding officers wore armour of the first type, and this was the most distinctive armour. The front portion of the armour extended to a point, and the wide-sleeved under-robe, the intricate armour plates and the elaborate design indicated the elevated rank of the wearer. A bright, tassled cape was worn at the shoulders. The simplest stye of armour also consisted of scales over a leather foundation. It is in fact very similar to the protection worn by a modern baseball catcher, where the front of the body is protected and the whole covering is held in placed by crossed straps at the back.

Ordinary infantrymen, charioteers and cavalry wore armour of the second type and this armour was adapted according to the rank and weaponry of the individual warrior. For the cavalrymen, the armour consisted of a short vest which was suitable for riding, being trim and efficient. The armour of the charioteers was more substantial and covered more of the body than any other soldier's armour. This armour had a neck guard and articulated sleeves to protect the arms without hindering movement. Armour composed of small plates in this manner had to be very complex if it was to allow the soldier to move as well as provide protection. In the charioteers' suits, for example, there are 323 separate plates which make up the covering.

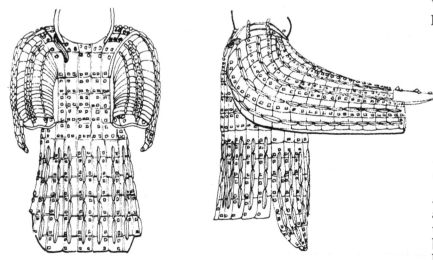

Most likely these plates were attached in such a way that they flexed or moved with the body. It appears from the armour of the clay warriors that the plates were joined together by nails. However, all of the plates could also have been joined by leather thongs, and in that case, the rivet-like bumps would simply be the knots of the thong.

Qin's War Machine

THE SOPHISTICATION OF THE QIN war machine is evident to us from the findings at Shihuang's tomb and from the literary sources we still have of the period. It is clear that this machine was the product of several centuries of development.

Qin had quickly realized that the expensive, heavy and slow chariots were not contributing to their campaigns, and as early as 644 B.C., there are indications that the state had switched extensively to cavalry and was flouting the rules of ceremonial warfare. With its long tradition of horse-breeding, Qin also enjoyed an advantage in this type of warfare.

Earlier, Qin had also realized the importance of reliable sources of manpower, and it was among the first of the states to impose universal conscription which made possible the astonishing size of its armies.

Lord Shang's division of the population into groups of five or ten families which were obliged to furnish a quota of fifteen-year-old conscripts, combined with the growth of Qin's population due to the state's agricultural innovations, made possible a standing infantry force of one million men.

These men were virtually all rough peasants trained at an early age for battle. When they fought, their lighter armour and cavalry permitted the troops to out-manoeuvre the more traditionally outfitted soldiers of the other states who were still slowed down by their heavy armour and cumbersome chariots.

There were three other features of the Qin military machine that also contributed to their success.

First, Shang Yang's decree that only those who excelled in warfare should be accorded a life of luxury, neatly created a professional military class. It also held out to the more lowly a chance to rise rapidly in the social and economic hierarchy. Those who so succeeded developed an intense loyalty to the state.

Secondly, failure or insubordination in the army was not tolerated. Many generals were demoted or executed after they failed to live up to expectations, including the mighty Bai Qi, a successful general for thirty-five years and the man responsible for the great victory over Zhao in 260 B.C. When he refused to command an invasion in 258 B.C. because he thought it was doomed to failure, instead of receiving respect for his experienced military judgement, he was demoted to the rank of common soldier, and after suffering this indignity, was executed.

Thirdly, the state often used generals who had risen from obscure origins, or had even come from other states. One example was Fan Sui, a native of Wei, who rose to high position in Qin by formulating that strategy whereby Qin formed alliances with distant states while concentrating on the conquest of those nearby.

His astute counsel lasted for fifteen years until two generals he had recommended to posts of command surrendered in battle and Fan Sui was summarily dismissed. In Qin law, the failure of one's protegés also meant punishment for the sponsor. Warfare in the state of Qin was so important that not even a single error would be forgiven.

Spies and intelligence were also extremely important in the victories of Qin. There are numerous stories of troops made to look unprepared and sloppy in order to lull the enemy into a false sense of security.

One despatch from the field reads:

"They [the enemy] are stopping up the wells with mud. They all got into their chariots and now the men on the left and right have taken their weapons and got down. They are listening to the order of their commander.

"Will they fight? I cannot tell yet."

One of the first of the Warring States to practise universal conscription, Qin forced thousands of peasants to join their war machine.

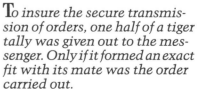

To insure the secure transmission of orders, one half of a tiger tally was given out to the messenger. Only if it formed an exact fit with its mate was the order carried out.

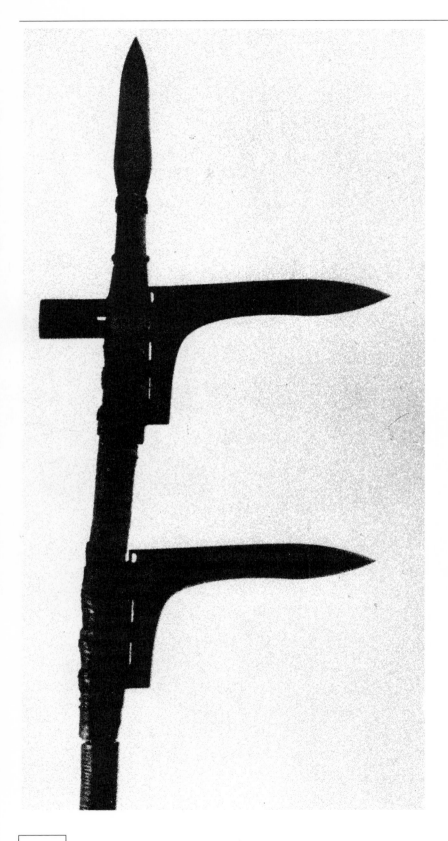

Weapons

Because warfare was central to the Warring States Period, many bronze weapons had been cast in the years before the short-lived Qin dynasty was established. Of these, a large percentage were inscribed, and from these inscriptions we can see that the weapons were cast either by the central government or were products of a local foundry. These inscriptions also tell us other interesting information, such as the date of the weapon's manufacture. All of this helps us to piece together a picture of life and society in the days of the first emperor.

The more than ten thousand real weapons unearthed from the pits of the terracotta army give a clear picture of the use and development of weapons, and the stage of metallurgy in Qin China. Ironically, however, the fact that the clay army was buried with real weapons has meant that the tombs were pillaged by later dynasties for military supplies. A number of different weapon types were used in the Qin period, including swords, crossbows, bows, halberds, long- and short-handled spears and pikes.

All of the weapons are finely made, indicating that the Qin possessed advanced metal-working technology. The vast majority of the weapons are made of cast bronze, which is an alloy of copper and tin. In some cases, there are traces of other metals such as nickel, bismuth, zinc and silicon. The percentages of metals were varied according to the type of armament being cast, so as to best suit the weapon for its purpose. Swords, for example, had a tin content of 21%, which refined the texture and increased the hardness comparable to that of tempered carbon steel. Arrowheads, on the other hand, had less tin but more lead, roughly 7%. The addition of the dense, heavy lead to the arrowhead alloy would increase its mass and therefore its impact on its target, and the lead, being relatively inexpensive, would help to "stretch" the more costly bronze alloy. This implies that Qin metal workers were able to control the proportions of the metals in the alloys they produced, thus demonstrating a knowledge of the properties of metals which enabled the Qin to make advances in military power.

Stacked on a pole, dagger axes and halberds proved to be formidable weapons.

Remarkably enough, in spite of having been buried for two thousand years, the swords found in the pits are for the most part uncorroded, and many of them are clean, shiny, and still able to split a hair. Weapons found near the mausoleum of Qin Shihuang appear to have undergone some type of anti-corrosion treatment. Scientific analysis of these weapons reveals a very dense oxide layer, and suggests that the methods used by the Qin metal workers involved the use of chrome on the surface of the weapons, a method not discovered by Europeans until the 1930s.

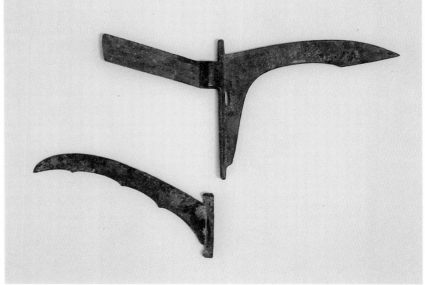

These two slender blades were cast in bronze.

Weapons ...

Crossbows, judging by the large number of bronze trigger mechanisms unearthed in the pits, seem to have been more common in the Qin than they had been earlier. Although few fragments of the wooden bodies of these crossbows remain, archaeologists are able to reconstruct the crossbow. It seems that originally, these Qin crossbows were painted red. Introduced to warfare in the mid-Warring States Period, the crossbow was a deadly weapon, much more powerful than any other type of armament at that time, and capable of piercing armour at great distances. Unlike the long bow, which was drawn by the archer's arm, the crossbow was set by mechanical means, and therefore could be drawn to a much greater tension. Wooden bows were also reinforced with an extra layer of wood to increase their resiliency and power. The crossbow was fired with a trigger mechanism much like a gun. This trigger mechanism was cast in four separate pieces, a process which required great precision on the part of the bronze caster. The "bolts," or arrows, for the crossbows consisted of two separately made parts: the triangular heads and the circular shafts. Two bronze crossbow mechanisms and six quivers with 80-100 arrows apiece were found in the same trench as some of the clay figures.

A bronze crossbow mechanism

The swords carried by Qin soldiers were double-edged, and were carried in wooden scabbards when not in use. There were two general sizes, both of which were made from cast bronze. The longer of the two was narrow and tapering, with a long, plain hilt. The shorter was broader, less tapered, and had two rings on the hilt to provide a firmer grip for the warrior. The grip of both types could be made more secure by binding twine around the handle. Swords were not common, however, as they were carried only by cavalrymen, fighting charioteers and officers, and not the infantry who formed the bulk of the army.

One type of weapon carried by infantry was the *ge*, or halberd, which consisted of a dagger-shaped blade mounted across the top of a long wooden shaft. The shaft of this weapon, up to three metres in length, made it an even more deadly weapon than the sword, since it measurably increased the soldier's reach, enabling him to harm a sword-carrier while remaining out of reach.

A selection of bronze spearheads

◁ S*hihuang's army of Blackhaired peasants staunchly face their attackers.*

In discussing the weaponry of Qin, the question arises concerning the use of the iron sword. It has long been thought that the victory of the Qin over the other states was due to advanced iron technology which enabled the Qin warriors to use wrought-iron weapons in their campaigns against the other states, who were using inferior swords made of bronze. Archaeological finds, however, do not substantiate this. In fact, evidence from sites dating to the Warring States Period reveals a much greater proportion of bronze weapons than iron. Furthermore, the few iron pieces that were found were not from areas controlled by the Qin.

Weapons, however highly decorated, are instruments of destruction. The wise man will have nothing to do with them.

Mencius

Preparation for Battle

DESPITE THE INNOVATIONS that made Qin the most formidable state during Shihuang's reign, his generals followed well-established precedents in their conduct of battle, and before each engagement, diviners carried out the customary rituals in order to forecast the battle's outcome.

Studying the heavens for signs and portents, and addressing questions to the guardian spirits of the state, the diviners also "listened to the wind," a task carried out by blind men who were considered to be in tune with the cosmos.

The *Shiji* also speaks of the secret alliances that were made, and the confusion of an enemy's strategy by the formation of far-flung cabals. To encourage the troops to fight more savagely, the lines of retreat were sometimes cut off even before the battle began. Huge spy networks were employed, as well, to bring back crucial information about the enemy's tactics and covenants made with allies were often ignored once the battle began.

As the moment of battle approached, the emphasis switched to provocation or flouting of the enemy. Hot-headed young warriors often delighted in provoking an attack by foolhardy displays of bravado.

Designed to impress the enemy with their spirit and readiness to fight, these displays might take the form of a daring rush into the enemy ranks in order to kill an officer and cut off his ear. Such acts were rewarded by the state of Qin with a promotion in rank and before each battle, generals sometimes even chose a particular "hero" to provoke the opposition.

*B*anners flying, drums pounding, the Qin cavalry plunges into battle.

The lower ranks—the bulk of the fighting force—performed the usual rituals of preparation for battle, sharpening their weapons, and watering the horses while they listened to their officers exhorting them to fight well.

It was not uncommon even for generals to walk among their men on the eve of battle and to send back to their homes the sick and the very young, thus demonstrating their wisdom and compassion for the individual soldier which, it was hoped, would inspire loyalty among the men under them.

The soldiers were sometimes told to level the cooking areas and burn their sleeping blankets. On the one hand, this cleared the chosen field of action, and on the other, hammered home the simple proposition that there would be no turning back from the battle that lay ahead.

Meanwhile the covert activities that were part of the preparations for every battle continued. Troops were advanced and brought back without actually engaging the enemy; fires were lit and then extinguished in order to deceive the enemy about their position; spies and deserters crossed the lines, back and forth, and were welcomed by either side, and any minute detail that might prejudice the outcome, such as the sickness of an officer, was kept secret.

Finally, ringing declarations of hostility were made, each carefully formed in classical language which condemned the enemy and justified the oncoming battle. Then the drums and gongs filled the air with a wild clamor, the state banners flew, the troops hurled themselves into the fray and the battle was joined. There would be no quarter given, and no mercy shown.

Another tactic of war was flouting the enemy and one account tells of 300 Qin chariots being paraded before the army of Chu with each chariot leader neatly doffing his cap to the enemy as it slowly rolled by. Designed as a mockery of a royal salute, the insult seemed to work for the Chu strategists sniffed,

"*The army of Qin is frivolous and lacking in propriety; they will surely be defeated. If they are frivolous, then they are deficient in wise counsel. If they lack propriety, then they are careless.*

"*If they carelessly get into a tight place and are deficient in counsel as well, can they escape defeat?*"

As it turned out, they could and did.

Chariots, Horses and the Cavalry

During the Shang Dynasty (c. 1765-1027 B.C.) and throughout most of the Zhou dynasty (1027-256 B.C.), the war chariot was a principal weapon of war. Historical records tell of many battles in which large numbers of chariots were involved. For example, a battle between the states of Qi and Jin in 589 B.C. involved some 800 chariots and 12,000 troops. The chariots of the Zhou period were ornamented with fine bronze fittings such as axle-caps and linch-pins, and were sumptuously inlaid with gold and silver. Large and difficult to manoeuvre, this symbol of strength and military authority required open country with flat, dry expanses of land for it to be useful, making the chariot an impractical vehicle for the rough terrain battles of the Warring States Period.

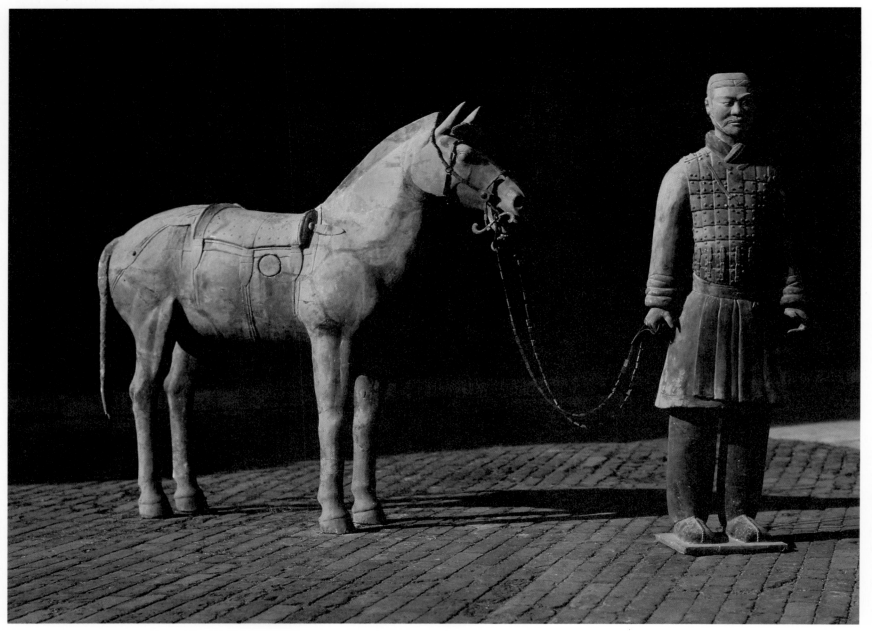

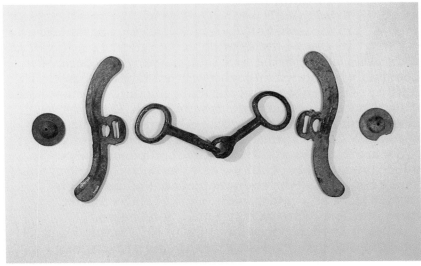

Bronze bridle fittings.

Because the war chariots buried in the pits were made of wood, only small pieces of them have survived the long entombment. However, extant bronze trappings, odd wooden fragments and imprints in the earth yield enough of the picture to allow us to reconstruct these Qin chariots. They were almost square in plan, measuring 1.3 to 1.5 metres wide and 1.2 metres long with an openwork balustrade around the vehicle which was open at the back to allow for entry. The charioteer held on to a raised horizontal bar across the front when driving. The two wheels were 1.8 metres in diameter. Planking covered the floor, and the chariot was adorned with geometric designs painted in lacquer.

Each chariot was drawn by a team of four thick-set and sturdy horses set four abreast, whose yokes were attached to the chariot by means of a single shaft. The innermost horses had yokes in the shape of an inverted "V" while leather traces connected the two outside horses.

In Pit 2, the numbers of chariot teams and cavalry are about equal. This suggests that the armies of the Qin had not yet fully embraced the notion of mounted warfare, since in succeeding periods, there were proportionally more cavalry. In battle formation, the chariots were concentrated close to the infantrymen, while the cavalry were placed along the periphery, so as to take maximum advantage of their greater mobility. The cavalrymen were armed with swords and crossbows.

The horses in the pits came complete with bridles. The bridle consisted of a two-part snaffle bit with rings at each end into which S-scroll guides were inserted and could slide easily. The tops and bottoms of these guides connected to the headstall straps. Two pendants hang from the snaffle bit rings; and the reins are attached to these. The headstall and the reins are made of bronze wire.

Although they were only a portion of the force, cavalry were nonetheless important to the Qin armies. The riders were practically dressed in trousers with shorter tunics; gone were the long Chinese robes, which could only hinder movement. The saddles, made of leather and metal and decorated with ribbons, were secured on top of the saddle blanket by a girth strap and a crupper. Stirrups were not to be used for another five centuries. When buried, the saddles were painted red, white, red-brown and blue.

According to the *Shiji*, cavalry were used in Zhou China by the troops of King Wu Ling of Zhao state (reigned 325-299 B.C.). When mounted tribesmen threatened the northern borders of his territory, he ordered his troops to adopt the horseback riding and mounted archery which were practiced by the nomadic peoples. Saddle horses with mounted warriors were far more mobile than the chariots and they could handle uneven ground. By the 3rd to 2nd centuries B.C., therefore, the chariot took a lesser role in tactics and served only as a symbol of power and authority.

Qin's Leadership

ALTHOUGH THE MILITARY MACHINE was the finest in the land, Qin also enjoyed another advantage over its rivals — its location in the valley of the Wei River. Defence of the state was relatively easy because it could only be entered through a very few strategic passes. The fertility of the irrigated soil prevented flooding — a curse of the central states — and farm yields were stable. The army was also in a constant state of readiness because of the need to constantly defend against the raids of maurading nomads.

But above all, it was the intangible components of power which brought about Qin's success. Between the time of Shang Yang's reforms and the enthronement of Shihuang, Qin enjoyed leadership under rulers of talent and competence, many of whom enjoyed exceptionally long reigns.

Three dukes held power for a total of 107 years and kept in force the early reforms of Shang Yang, widely recruiting for civil and military officers and rejuvenating the state again and again with new people, new thoughts and up-to-date statecraft. These rulers valued the art of diplomacy as highly as they did war to achieve their ends. They used threats, bribery and strategic alliances with consummate skill. Unlike some of the other states, in the century before Shihuang's rule there is no uprising recorded in Qin.

Twenty years before Shihuang became the king of Qin, the philosopher Xun Zi remarked:

"Qin's frontier defences are mountainous, its geographical configurations are beneficial. It has mountains, forests, streams and valleys and its natural resources are abundant. Thus in its geographical advantages, it is outstanding.

"Entering its frontiers and observing its customs, I saw that its people were simple and unsophisticated. Their music was not corrupting or licentious, nor was their clothing frivolous.

"They stood in deep awe of the officials and are people who follow the old customs obediently. When I entered the cities and towns, I saw that their officials were dignified and there were none who were not courteous, temperate, honest, sincere and tolerant. Their officials are worthy men."

Later, when Shihuang came to power and turned to his principal adviser, Li Si, to debate the philosophies of the early thinkers, Li Si was more abrupt and to the point. His simple analysis was:

"For four generations now, Qin has won victory. Its armies are the strongest in the world and its authority sways the other feudal lords. It did not reach this position by benevolence and righteousness, but by taking advantage of its opportunities.

"That is all."

In the 130-year history of Qin warfare (364-234 B.C.), the *Shiji* lists fifteen battles and in all but one instance, the enemy casualties were never less than 20,000.

In four of these battles, 100,000 dead opponents are listed. The heaviest death toll appears to have happened in 260 B.C. in the campaign against Zhao when the *Shiji* records that Zhao lost 50,000 men. The army of 400,000 then surrendered and was massacred except for 240 who were allowed to return.

The combined casualties allegedly inflicted by Qin on its rivals during the 130 years amounts to 1,489,000.

Qin's military machine was the finest in the land.

Shihuang's Early Campaigns

WHEN HE CAME TO THE THRONE in 246 B.C., Shihuang found himself king of a state pulsing with energy and ready to take advantage of all military opportunities. Shihuang missed none of them.

As soon as he reached adulthood, he started his march across the land. Unfortunately, the chronicles of the *Shiji* are little more than lists of battles in which Qin was victorious, but it was obvious that he increased the military activity of his state in the drive for conquest.

His standing army remained honed and ready for combat as Shihuang subtly shifted Qin from a state holding the balance

There were seven states in China during the Warring States Period which were major contenders for supremacy: Qi, Yan, Zhao, Han, Wei, Qin and Chu.

The tales of war from the *Shiji* often illustrate the codes of chivalry, especially this one involving an incident between Jin and Chu at the great battle of Pi.

One Jin chariot got stuck in a rut as it was retiring from the field of warfare and a courteous Chu soldier came along and advised the Jin commander on how to lighten the chariot and get it out of the mud-hole.

Obviously upset, the Jin warrior snarled at the enemy benefactor: *"We cannot equal your great state in the number of times we have run away."*

Shihuang's vast army swept across the land on their drive for conquest.

of power in a savage land to a fierce principality preparing to bring the rest of the states under its heel.

Shihuang now sent out a new generation of generals in a series of wide-ranging campaigns. They were led by Meng Ao, whose son, Meng Tian, later became the architect of the Great Wall. In the first years of Shihuang's reign, Qin conquered the two border states on the east, Wei and Zhao.

This was a direct retaliation for an invasion of Qin in 241 B.C. When Wei and Zhao, aware of the growing threat to their security that Qin posed, had sent their enemies against Shihuang's, their invasion was quickly put down, and they suffered more than 400,000 casualties.

At that time, military strategy in Qin was being guided by the regent, Lu Buwei, aided perhaps by the queen's lover, Lao Ai. Historians of the period, while acknowledging that the policies were sound, also record a number of unfavourable omens such as a plague of locusts, untimely comets and famine in Qin. These are historical conventions, intended to suggest that Qin would be victorious but that the cost to the people would be high.

The Wars of Unification

FROM THE TIME SHIHUANG became King of Qin in 246 B.C., Qin was, like her neighbours, constantly at war. But these conflicts were shapeless and inclusive, with the advantage see-sawing back and forth. It was not until after he assumed his majority in 238 B.C., and until Li Si began to offer his counsel that the conquest began to take shape and the overall strategy of Qin became apparent.

The first step was to strengthen his economic base with further colonization in the southwest. Four thousand households were transported there in 237 B.C., while he temporarily secured his eastern flank with huge bribes, of 300,000 pieces of gold to influential ministers of the various states in order to prevent alliances against Qin. Then, using two of the finest generals of the age, Wang Qian and Huan I, he began a series of probing attacks against his nearest neighbours. The states of Zhao, Han and Wei, victims of successive defeats by Qin, were forced to cede to Shihuang more and more territory. Bribes, espionage and fear kept the more distant states from coming to the aid of their threatened neighbours, and no grand alliance was formed against Qin.

In 231 B.C., a grand force was mobilized in Qin and the real work of conquest began. First to fall, in 230 B.C. was the state of Han, its king captured, and all its territory turned into a single commandery of Qin. Two years later, Zhao, which had been the most persistent of Qin's foes was also annexed, and after Wang Qian's great victory there, Shihuang left his own palace and travelled to Handan, the fallen capital of Zhao. This was the home of his mother, and there he coldly supervised the murder of all those who had mistreated her in her younger days. He had a long memory and always avenged wrongs against either him or his family.

The inexorable march of Qin to the east, caused the ruler of Yan, in desperation, to send Jing Ke on his ill-fated assassination attempt on Shihuang, and the next year, 226 B.C., he lost his capital and his life to Wang Qian's forces. In 222 B.C., the state of Yan was extinguished.

Wei fell in 225 B.C., when a ruthless Qin general destroyed the dikes of the river on which its capital stood, and flooded the city, causing a vast number of casualties.

Now there remained only the battered and weakened state of Qi in the northeast, a truncated Yen, and Qin's most formidable foe, the powerful southern state of Chu. Perceiving little threat in the north, Shihuang forced his veteran general Wang Qian, out of retirement, and placed him in charge of an army said to number 600,000. His invasion was bloody but successful, and once again, Shihuang left his own capital to survey his newest acquisition. Chu, however, refused to accept his rule, and Wang Qian was forced to suppress one last, great uprising before the state was annexed in 223 B.C.

Yan fell in 222 B.C., and then only Qi stood, beleaguered and alone. Once the most powerful of the states, and possessor of a proud tradition, its king put up what small resistance he could, but it was fruitless. Shihuang sent one of his agents to invite the king to come to Qin and surrender, offering him large land grants and an honourable retirement. The king agreed, and in 221 B.C., made his sad progress to Qin, and there, was immediately imprisoned and starved to death.

China, at great cost, was at last united.

▷ *The empire unified.*

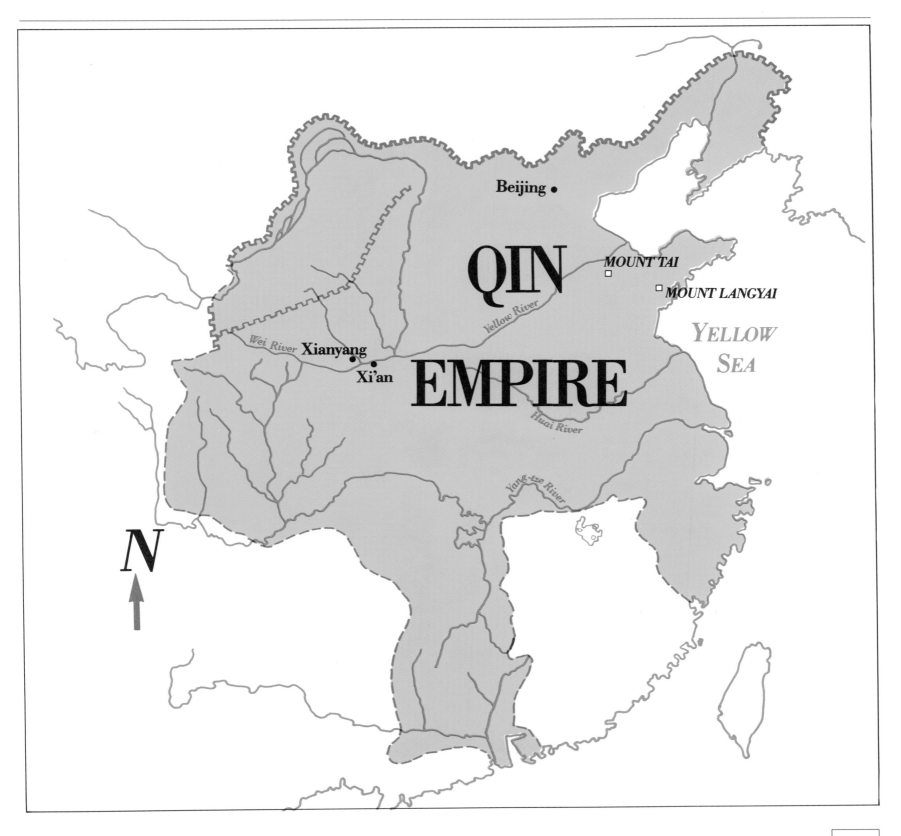

QIN
EMPIRE

Beijing •

MOUNT TAI □

□ MOUNT LANGYAI

YELLOW
SEA

Yellow River

Wei River Xianyang
• Xi'an

Huai River

Yang-tze River

N

An Imperfect Peace

THE SPEED OF THE UNIFICATION and the number of Shihuang's conquests is astounding. After five centuries of division, China had been united by twenty-five years of war. The most populous of the world's nations now owed its allegiance to one ruler, the "Tiger Emperor."

The peasants who formed the army thought that what they most wanted had been finally achieved: They could return home to work their fields in peace and establish their families. They rejoiced, believing the time had now come when, laying down their crossbows and halberds, they could take up their scythes and work their farms.

But Shihuang did not allow them to rest. Instead of permitting the peasants to return to their fields, he was soon to use vast numbers of them as a construction force to build his roads, palaces, canals, and the Great Wall.

Despite his promises he did not end war. Although the inscriptions he left on the mountain tops always made reference to the peace he had brought to the land, the battles never ended. He continued to fight, either to hold his nomadic foes at bay, or to win new territories in the southeastern part of the land. Eventually Shihuang's territory stretched almost to the borders of Viet Nam.

Shihuang's ambitions would not allow him to stop and his visions for his new empire were far more important to him, finally, than the happiness of his Blackhaired people. The *Shiji* tells of military campaigns long after unification and the so-called peace. General Meng Tian was ordered to build the road network and the Great Wall while at the same time thousands of troops were deployed along the outer borders to hold back the barbarians.

These troops, who were sometimes conscripted from distant parts of the country and forced to leave their homes and families, became bewildered and angry at the never-ending labour. And there was no question of their disobeying — the fierce punishments meted out to all who rebelled saw to that.

Many thousands of soldiers also died while constructing the Great Wall. While an honourable death on the field of battle might have been acceptable, death caused by the unremitting labour and harsh working conditions far from their homes was not — and for one very important reason: Burial without the performance of the proper family rituals condemned the dead to wander eternally as "hungry ghosts."

Shihuang failed, fatally, as it later turned out, to recognize the distinction between "obtaining and maintaining" an empire, or as Qin's first critic, Jia Yi more graphically put it:

"On the back of a horse, one might win an empire, but can one govern that empire without dismounting?"

Shihuang often erected stelae, upright stone slabs decorated with inscriptions, promising the peace he had brought to all the land.

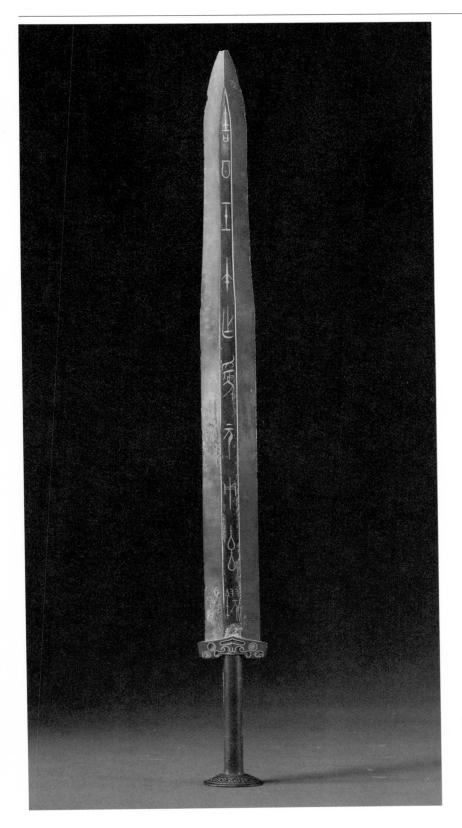

In the time of the Warring States, a battle between Chu and Wei was marked by the seizing of the Wei king's sacred vessel, a talisman carried into all the Wei battles. The Wei general pointed out to his army that the loss of the sacred vessel was an offence so grave they would all be eventually killed, so they decided to retrieve it.

Going through the ranks, they selected three men with long beards who looked slightly like the warriors of Wei and sent them by night into the camp of the victorious Chu who were now feasting and dancing to celebrate their victory.

As the three impostors did not know the password, they were killed but their supporting force managed to retrieve the vessel and even though Chu won the original battle, the *Shiji* historians recorded it as a hollow victory because the talisman of Wei was recovered.

The rallying cry and the boosting of the troops' morale played an important part in pre-battle psychology. No one did better than the generals of Qin. One handled it this way by walking through his quivering forces on the eve of battle and announcing:

"Let the old and the young return home. Send back single sons and the sick. Where there are two soldiers of one family, *let one return. Select your weapons and look to your carriages. Feed your horses and have a good meal.*

"When the army has been marshalled, burn your resting places. Tomorrow we shall fight."

It worked. The army cheered the action and the loss of a few hundred men was more than offset by the new vigor of the Qin troops.

This long and slender bronze sword, which dates between the eighth and the fifth centuries B.C., has an inscription inlaid with gold concerning its date of manufacture.

統一

UNIFICATION

ALL UNDER HEAVEN

The Unification of China

The Symbolism of the Qin Dynasty

IMMEDIATELY AFTER RECORDING the fall of Qi, the last of the Warring States to be conquered by Shihuang, the *Shiji* tersely remarks: " ... And now Qin possessed "All under Heaven."

The next passage in the *Shiji* contains a speech by Shihuang justifying each of his conquests on the basis of the bad faith of his rivals. Attributing his success to the virtue of his ancestors, he then demands that his ministers suggest for him a new title, one commensurate with his great deeds, so that they might be transmitted to later generations. Clearly, he sought a title which would set him apart from all earlier rulers, since, as one of his sycophantic ministers remarked, his achievements surpassed those of all his predecessors, including even the legendary sage-kings of antiquity.

After some deliberation, he made the choice himself.

He announced that he would henceforth be known as "August Emperor" or *huangdi. Huang* was a term previously used for a series of three legendary culture-heroes, and *di* had sacred associations of even greater import, having been used to address the supreme deity more than a thousand years before. The *shi* of his title meant "first" for his dynasty would endure, he said, "for generations without end." The overall effect of his new title was that Shihuang had made himself almost superhuman.

Nor did he lose any time in transforming the symbolism of his regime.

At that time a certain theory existed called the Five Elements or Five Phases. According to it, fire, water, earth, wood and metal succeeded each other in an endless cycle, each destroying its predecessor to give a dominant character to its age. The wise ruler harnessed the dominant element and used it along with its associated colour and number to legitimize his reign. Since the Zhou dynasty had ruled by the virtue of fire, Shihuang chose water as his element, the colour black for his court robes, pennants and flags, and the number six, the water number, as the standard measurement for such things as caps, axle-widths and even a man's regular "pace." He re-named his people "the Blackhaired ones," and since water was considered a cold and harsh element, he determined that his law would also be harsh and repressive and his rule, severe. "For a long time," remarks the *Shiji*, "there were no amnesties."

With his own position now suitably elevated, and that of his regime secure, Shihuang next set out to transform China.

It is difficult to imagine the magnitude of the tasks he set for himself, for we must remember that the conquest had been swift. Each of the proud states he had brought to their knees possessed its own valued traditions and might easily rise up again if these were threatened. Hundreds of thousands of men, all experienced soldiers, existed in the defeated states, along with the royal families who had been their rulers.

What should Shihuang do with these potential threats to his rule?

"water"

"black"

"six"

The element water was associated with the colour black and the number 6.

"winter"

There was a widespread belief that the guardian element of the dynasty preceding Qin was fire. Qin's choice of water was dictated by the fact that water extinguishes fire just as the Qin dynasty toppled the House of Zhou.

The Rejection of Feudalism

Shihuang had the bronze weapons of the captives melted and twelve massive statues cast. These were later melted down for coins.

NEVER INDECISIVE, SHIHUANG moved rapidly to make sure that the defeated aristocrats would be rendered powerless. We are told that he immediately moved 120,000 of the "rich and powerful" families away from their old homes, and brought them to Xianyang where he constructed for them new palaces, perhaps in the style of their former homes – a marvelous architectural feat! The weapons of the demobilized troops, except for those of the Qin soldiers, were collected and melted down, we are told, to make bronze bells and twelve, almost unbelievably huge statues, each weighing nearly thirty tons. These statues, probably guardian figures, adorned the palace courtyard for almost four-hundred years, until at the end of the Han dynasty, they were, in turn, melted down.

There was more behind these moves by Shihuang than just the purely tactical. Certainly it made sense to keep potential enemies under close surveillance in the capital, and to remove the weapons of their supporters. However, what a grand conceit it was, for the new emperor to embellish his city with the tone and the lavish lifestyle of the former aristocrats and to embellish his palace with the awe-inspiring statues. Never before in China had there been such a capital!

The *Shiji*, after relating the territorial extent of the new empire, tells us that it was a time of great celebration – perhaps the equivalent of "peace in our time" among ordinary people. In the capital area, the replicas of the palaces of captured states were constructed, and, "...*in court after court, there were walled-in walkways and covered galleries, one after the other. Here were kept the beautiful women and the musical instruments captured from other states.*"

After this period of rejoicing, Shihuang now moved on to his most serious reforms, the first of which was to politically cement his unification.

The manner in which he chose to do this is interesting. Not only does it show his acumen, his decisiveness, and willingness to discard precedent, but it also shows his vision for a new China.

In 221 B.C., the conquest now complete, his Chancellor, Wang Guan, suggested that the more distant states could not be effectively governed from Xianyang. He advocated the restoration of the Zhou system of feudal investiture, with Shihuang's sons ennobled and given charge of these more distant units.

His view, however, was immediately challenged by his junior officer, Li Si. He argued brilliantly that the Zhou example had proven to be disastrous and had led to nothing but strife, which the Zhou ruler had become increasingly unable to prevent. Skillfully appealing to Shihuang's vanity, he reminded him that "his divine might" had given him possession of the whole world. Did he intend, the implication was, to be less than all-powerful, and to weaken the unity he had forged at so great a cost? Li Si argued that state revenues and other rich rewards would be enough to content the princes of Qin as well as the generals and officials who had aided in the conquest. All power, however, should remain in the emperor's hands.

Agreeing with Li Si's argument, Shihuang did not hesitate to remind all his ministers that it was his conquest that had brought, at long last, a respite from war. There would be no more armies in the land, he told them and decreed that "All under Heaven" be divided into thirty-six administrative units called commanderies, with each further subdivided into counties. In each commandery, there were stationed three representatives of the central government – a Civil Governor (*shou*), a Military Governor (*wei*) and an Imperial Overseer or Inspector (*jian-yu-shi*).

No longer was government in the hands of aristocrats. These officials were appointed for their ability, and while the division of responsibility among the three is not so clear as we might like, we do know that the offices were salaried, non-hereditary, and held only for a period determined by the throne. The Overseer, moreover, seems to have been akin to a personal representative of the emperor, which guaranteed tight imperial control and created a system of checks-and-balances so that no provincial official became too powerful. Each country was also governed by a centrally-appointed magistrate.

The system was not a Qin innovation, nor was Shihuang the first ruler to apply it. He did, however, refine it and was, of course, the first to apply it universally. It was adopted with some modification by the following dynasty, the Han, and became the ancestor of the provincial system still used in China today. Its real importance, however, lies in the fact that it provided an alternative to the looseness of "feudal" administration and made China one of the world's first centralized bureaucracies. Henceforth, the educated administrator would increasingly supplant the warrior as the dominant figure in society, and the imperial institution would be immensely strengthened.

The centralization of political power in the cause of unity is perhaps Shihuang's greatest accomplishment.

The Standardization of Chinese Script

STILL FLUSHED WITH SUCCESS, the First Emperor turned his attention to an important priority – the imposition of a greater degree of cultural unity. It has only been in recent years that the astonishing cultural variety and regional differences which existed in the Chinese culture prior to unification have been revealed to us through archaeology. Each region had distinctive characteristics in artistic expression and folk customs, in the use of bronze and iron technology, in the type of agricultural implements and land use, in weaponry, in coinage, in weights and measures, in burial practices, in systems of ranks and titles, and even in script.

To bring about total cultural unity was a monumental, perhaps impossible task – and no Chinese dynasty has ever succeeded in doing it. Shihuang, however, would make great strides.

For the First Emperor, far and away the most urgent task lay in the area of communication. Just as today, when the speech of a man from, say, Hong Kong is largely incomprehensible to a man from Beijing, so too, in those early times, there must have been marked dialectical differences from state to state.

The sage-king Fuxi, the originator of Chinese script.

Moreover, and unlike today, the same word was often represented by a different character or pictograph, depending on the time it was written and probably to a lesser extent, on the region in which it was found. Though only a tiny proportion of the population was literate, the lack of a systematic script not only made inaccessible any common literary heritage, but vastly impeded the work of the government.

Again, Shihuang took swift action. The annals of the First Emperor in the *Shiji* record that in the very year of unification, and even before the wealthy families were brought to the capital, "the script was unified," a laconic phrase that tells us little.

Another section of the same work, which attributes the reform to Li Si, adds that the new characters were "made universal in the Empire," but provides no further details, so once again we must have recourse to archaeology. There is an extensive literature on the subject, and recent research seems to agree that the process of reform was primarily a matter of simplifying the complexities of earlier script and suppressing variant forms of the same word. Later tradition, probably unreliable, attributes to Li Si, a dictionary of the newly-standardized forms consisting of 3,300 characters.

The effects of this standardization of the script cannot be over-estimated. Although it must have taken some years to be put into effect, the Qin "Small-seal" script and its offshoot, the "clerk" style, provided the standard for all further evolution of the written Chinese language. It lent itself, too, to graceful expression, especially as the use of the writing brush – an invention traditionally but erroneously ascribed to Shihuang's general Meng Tian – became more widespread. Calligraphy was to become the most respected of the Chinese arts, the foundation of Chinese painting, and an important element in the attainment of an official career!

So elegant and so strangely efficient was this written language, that its pictographical aspect could add a deeper dimension to Chinese poetry as easily as it could provide an astonishing force and economy to Chinese prose. As time passed the language became more complex and the number of characters proliferated, reaching about 80,000 in the famous *Kangxi* dictionary of the eighteenth century. Yet not until the twentieth century were there serious calls for replacement of characters with an alphabet. The solution since 1949 has been to simplify the form of the characters and to restrict the number in common use – echoing with some precision, the very solution chosen by Shihuang.

But dwarfing all the other effects of the reform is one single fact: The standardization of the written language held China together.

殷商甲骨			
西周銅銘			
春秋戰國銘 秋國刻			
秦楷 篆書			

To the Chinese, writing (wen) had extraordinary significance. The first of the legendary culture heroes, Fuxi, had been the inventor, inspired by the markings on the back of a mystical turtle who emerged from the Yellow River before his eyes. The sage-king known as the Yellow Emperor, a very popular figure in the Qin culture, had first systematized the script. The Chinese word for "culture" (wen-hua) means literally "to transform by writing," and the word for "civilization" (wen-ming), means "to make brilliant by writing." In short, the written word was the measure and the marker of societal and individual attainment, and a transcendental gift from highest antiquity.

The three Chinese characters pictured here from left to right are dragon, horse and bird. This chart shows the gradual evolution of the Chinese script from the most ancient time to our modern standard style with the earliest style, the oracle bone script, shown at the top. Today's characters are at the bottom of the chart.

Ancient Chinese Thought

THE AGE INTO WHICH SHIHUANG was born was both philosophically and religiously eclectic, a time of intellectual ferment during which rapid social mobility brought the rawest forms of folk belief into the upper levels of society at the same time that their own elevated and agnostic moralism filtered gradually down into the hut of the meanest peasant. It was a time of confusion, a time when differing ideologies competed for primacy every bit as fiercely as the bloodthirsty states competed in war. It was also a time when the greatest struggle was between those loyal to the past, those who harboured a nostalgic vision of restoring the Golden Age of the legendary sage-kings, and their rivals, those who had long tired of this "vain and empty" longing for a long-gone utopia. And they were ready and eager to deal with present-day realities and crash headlong into the future.

Shihuang was one of the latter, a realist interested in the solutions for his own period of time and the legacy he would leave for future generations of the Qin Dynasty. While he was conversant with all the currents of thought in his time, and demonstrated an astonishing ability to blend and use them to validate his actions, his greatest loyalty was to the new, the novel and the first. Never would he lose sight of the fact that he was the first to unite his country and, therefore, had the right to make himself the First Emperor of China. And that meant rejecting the past, rejecting the constant and irritating calls with which his scholars frequently plagued him: "Restore the feudal system of feoffdoms!" "Learn from the books of the past!" "Place your government in the hands of trusted ministers!" "Rule by virtue and benevolence, not harsh law. For these are the ways of the sages, and their rules were long!" But Shihuang ignored them and, instead, concentrated on the words of his most influential teacher, Han Feizi:

...And there was once a man of the [state of] Song who tilled his field. In the midst of his field stood the stump of a tree, and one day a hare, running at full speed, bumped into the stump, broke its neck and died. Thereupon the man left his plow and kept watch at the stump, hoping that he would get another hare. But he never caught another hare, and was only ridiculed by the people of Song. Now those who try to rule the people of the present age with the conduct of government of the early kings are all doing exactly the same thing...

History does not repeat itself, contended Feizi, and more than anything else, it was Shihuang's grasp of that essential fact which made him the First Emperor of China.

He was almost alone among the rulers of the time in acting on this belief, for the rest gave their allegiance to the solutions proposed by one or more of the so-called "Hundred Schools," or more commonly, the "Hundred Flowers," which had bloomed only a few centuries before.

Buddhism did not appear in China until the first century A.D. This is a representation of Guanyin, the Deity of Compassion.

◁*Few people realize that the historic Buddha was a near contemporary of Confucius.*

Confucius and the Chinese Classics

THE FIFTH CENTURY B.C. was a remarkable time in China, just as it was in other centres of the civilized world. In China, we associate the great efflorescence of thought, the outpouring of guiding values for whole civilizations, with the name of Confucius, but other societies had their sages too. In India, it was the time of the historic Buddha, the systematization of the *vedas* and the *upanishads* and the foundation of Jain. And on the littoral of the Mediterranean world, we have the great Hebrew prophets of the Babylonian Captivity, the formulations of Zoroaster in the rising Persian Empire, and of course, the brilliance of the philosophers and mathematicians who adorned Periclean Athens. What was in the air in this fecund period of human endeavour?

In China, there was desperation in the air. Two centuries of internecine strife had devasted the land, had turned father against son and brother against brother, and had made the existence of state and individual so precarious, that the thinkers of the time had no interest in the abstract dialectic of the Greeks. And since centuries of appeal to Heaven and the faithful sacrifices of the Zhou kings had brought no respite, the patient predictions of a Hebrew Messiah and the first of the Buddha's Four Noble Truths, that "life is pain and illusion,"

Confucius, *the most important of all Chinese philosophers.*

held no appeal for them. Man's problems were to be solved by men, and thus the major Chinese schools of thought all had a decidedly humanistic cast. They taught that problems of this world should be solved by those *in* this world. Chinese thought, at that time, was thus far less "religious" than in many other parts of the contemporary world.

The first and greatest of the Chinese thinkers was called Confucius – the Latinized version of "Master Kong" (Kong Fuzi), as he was known when the Jesuits first arrived in China. His life, traditionally considered to be from 551-479 B.C., was an undramatic one and, perhaps in his own eyes, a failure. His *Shiji* biography tells us that his only sign of distinction as an infant was that he was born with a hollow in his head – perhaps the repository of his later wisdom! He was born into a decayed noble family, the son of an elderly father and his teen-aged secondary wife, so that he was orphaned while still a child. Somehow, perhaps by virtue of family tradition, he managed to gain an education, and held a relatively minor office in his native state of Lu in the northeast.

Either because he felt unappreciated there, or because his vision was a wider one, he set out to become one of the many roving scholars who sought to gain audience with the contending lords, and to advise them on how best to govern their people. But, says his biography, "he was dismissed from Qi, driven out of Song and Wei, and ran into trouble between Chen and Zai." Thus, anticipating the cliché, that "those who can, do; while those who can't do, teach", he returned to his native state of Lu and began to gather disciples about him.

Soon his reputation spread, and he was entrusted with higher state offices and with some delicate diplomatic missions. He was uncompromising in his devotion to rectitude, wholly devoted to the lessons of history, and of such commanding presence – the *Shiji* tells us he was nicknamed the "Tall Man" – that he enjoyed much success. He was clearly aware of the rising power of Qin, for in 521 BC., he remarked on the secret of Duke Mu of Qin's success: *"Small though it is, Qin aspires to great things. An outlying state, it follows the correct ways of behaviour. Duke (Mu) ransomed a slave with five sheepskins and after examining him for three days, entrusted to him the afffairs of state. For this reason, we may call him a king, not just a conqueror!"*

In the words of Confucius, there is often some meaning lying below the surface, and his statement here may have been a gentle rebuke to a lord who was not utilizing to the fullest the talents of Confucius himself. At the same time, though, and exactly three centuries before the unification, he knew that Qin "aspired to great things."

The so-called "Confucian Classics" became the canon and "Bible" of the Chinese people from the second century B.C. to the present day. The whole educational system and the civil service examinations were based on these works, and though they run to over 400,000 words, it was not uncommon for scholars to memorize them *in toto*.

Originally, there were six *Classics*, but the one concerned with music has disappeared. The others consist of the *Book of Changes*, a manual of divination; the *Book of History* which is concerned with the speeches and the deeds of the legendary sage-kings of antiquity; the *Book of Poetry* which contains over three hundred poems later interpreted as having hidden moral meaning; the *Spring and Autumn Annals*, a history of Confucius' home-state, and finally, the *Book of Ritual*, which regulates proper behaviour for everyone from the ruler to the meanest peasant.

Modern scholarship is dubious that these works ever had a direct connection with Confucius, but for twenty centuries, the Chinese regarded him as the author or editor of all of them.

Since most of them contained the message that the past was superior to the present, it is easy to see why Shihuang wanted to have them destroyed!

The Confucian classics formed the foundation of the Chinese educational system for over 2,000 years. Here, an elderly woman transmits the knowledge of the ages.

The Political Failure of Confucius

DURING THE NEXT DECADE, Confucius refined his thinking and seemed to have in prospect a fine career in Qi until one of his critics convinced the Duke there that he was an arrogant, self-willed "windbag," and that his emphasis on etiquette and ritual, and codes of behaviour were irrelevant to the serious work of state preservation and expansion. Back in his home state after this rebuff, Confucius began his great work of editing what became the *Chinese Classics*, six works (one no longer extant), which were to become the basis of the Chinese educational system and the Chinese value system from the second century B.C. until well into the twentieth century.

Although past fifty now, he was enticed once more into government service, and according to the *Shiji*, became chief miniser of Lu at the age of fifty-six, "delighting in his high position only because it gave him a chance to show his humility."

After only three months, his strengths as an administrator were so evident that the neighbouring state of Qi grew fearful of Lu's strength and sent, to seduce the duke, "eighty of her most beautiful dancing-girls and sixty pairs of dappled horses." Accepting the gifts against the advice of Confucius, the duke began to neglect the affairs of state, and Confucius left his service, reputedly singing a song which began:

The tongue of a woman
Costs a man his post,
And the words of a woman,
May cost a man his head.
Why not retire,
And spend one's years in peace?

He was later to remark, with a sigh, "Food and sex are [the motivating forces of] human nature."

Still optimistic that some prince would heed him, Confucius continued to travel, "like a stray dog," as he himself put it, for the next fourteen years. Finally, he was invited back to Lu along with the seventy-two close disciples who had accompanied him on his travels. Shihuang, though no admirer of Confucius, probably set up the institution of the seventy "scholars of wide learning" in direct imitation of this number!

Back in his own state, Confucius received no post, but continued to teach and edit the last of the *Classics* until his death at the age of seventy-three. His last words were a lament that "the world has long strayed from the True Way."

Confucius, in his robes of office as the Magistrate of the state of Lu overseeing the hunt.

▷ *In his own lifetime, Confucius received little honour. In later ages, lavishly decorated temples devoted to him dotted the Chinese landscape.*

The True Way of Confucius

TO THE TWENTIETH CENTURY Western mind, already familiar with similar ideas from Greek philosophy and Christianity, the philosophy of Confucius seems so undramatic that he hardly seems to deserve his reputation as the moulder of the Chinese tradition. In point of fact, China did not become "Confucian" until five centuries after his death, and certainly during the Qin dynasty, Confucianism was not the dominant strain of thought. If there was one single, paramount reason for this, it lay in the fact that Confucius was an idealist.

For Confucius, like the "religious" leaders of other traditions, the solution to troubled times lay in a return to virtue: conformity by all human beings to a moral and natural order, which he called the Tao, the Way. But the Tao was not easy to understand, and Confucius, therefore, advocated that his followers "respect what is above, but keep it at arm's length." He concentrated on making human beings virtuous and he defined goodness as the practice of *ren*, a particular virtue which is usually rendered as "humanity" or "benevolence." His own definitions, as found in his collected sayings, *The Analects*, equated *ren* with the simple phrase, "Love mankind." Sometimes he defined it as a combination of other virtues like generosity, diligence, courtesy and kindness, and at other times, with his negative formulation of the Golden Rule, "Do not do unto others what you would not have them do unto you."

Confucius' solution to the disorder of his era was not strikingly original even in his own times, and one contemporary, Mo Zi, advocated an even more "universal" love of others. Confucius, however, provided in specific terms, a blueprint of the process through which mankind could obtain true humanity.

Confucius took as his starting-point, the grand statement which now begins UNESCO's 1950 *Statement on Race* – "By

---

One of China's more famous tales of filial piety involved a peasant called Dong Yong, who the *Shiji* say, was born around A.D. 200. His family was so poor that Dong Yong raised the money for his father's funeral by selling himself as a bonded servant for "ten thousand cash."

But after the funeral, while Dong Yong was preparing to begin his life-long indenture, he met a woman who agreed to marry him despite his plight. She proved so diligent and devoted that during their first month together, she wove three hundred pieces of silk, enough to pay off the funeral expenses.

Dong Yong was astonished and happy until the woman told him she was not mortal. She was the star Chi Nu, the Weaving Maiden, sent by the Lord of Heaven as a reward for Dong's filial piety, she told him, and after making the startling announcement, she vanished into thin air.

nature, human beings are all alike." But he went on to say that it was "learning and practice" which set them apart. We, therefore, find much of the *Analects* devoted to education, both formal and informal. Because of his insistence that there could be no class distinctions in education, that a teacher should "lift one corner of the square and the student three corners," and that "learning without thinking is labour lost," he became the foremost educator in Chinese history. And his ideal curriculum – literature, poetry, music, ethics and history, was to give China, through the ages, an enormous respect for formal education and particularly for "humane" studies.

"Practice" meant for Confucius, a combination of the desire to become humane, and the discipline to maintain the virtue, not forgetting it "even for the space of a single meal." And he enjoined upon everyone three main modes of behaviour, which, he taught, would make people humane.

The first was the practice of "filial piety," a love and respect for parents and grandparents, which made the family, not the individual, the basic social unit. Through the love and harmony of the ideal family, each member would be prepared to go into a world in which "all within the four seas are brothers," he wrote. Respect for the aged was also Confucius' most radical departure from the values of his own age, for he knew that war was a young man's game, one which required strength and passion. He promoted, instead, the contemplation and wisdom which come only with age. Filial piety became in time the real hallmark of Chinese civilization, and it is interesting to note that even Shihuang, who happily burned the Confucian *Classics*, was not immune from its demands. After exiling his adulterous mother for the part she played in her lover's rebellion in 238 B.C., he was persuaded to bring her back to the capital and to treat her with respect when a minister warned that all the other states would oppose him if he did not do so.

"**F**ilial piety is the root of all virtue," Confucius, the great Chinese philosopher and teacher who lived from 551-479 B.C., taught, and respect for one's parents was, and still is, considered of great importance in China.

Many of China's legends and tales concern the love and duty owed to one's parents such as the following which concerns Meng Zong, an official of the Qin dynasty in the time of Shihuang.

It seems that Meng Zong was so devoted to his mother that in the middle of a snow storm he attempted to find bamboo shoots to make her favourite soup.

The task was hopeless but Zong dug into the snow and began to weep as his fingers stiffened and his hands began to freeze. His tears melted the snow and, the legend says, fresh bamboo shoots grew up which he collected and took home to his sick mother.

Filial piety is "*the way to heaven, the principle of earth, and the practical duty of man*," Confucius wrote.

The Political Beliefs of Confucius

THE SECOND ASPECT of Confucian "Practice" is a principle called the "rectification of names" – "a father is a father, and a son is a son, a ruler is a ruler, and a subject is a subject." Tomes of scholarship have discussed this principle, but its practical meaning is clear. Confucius believed the root cause of disorder was greed, which made people fight to gain something to which they were not entitled. Hence, large states annexed their weaker neighbours and ambitious sons usurped the positions of their fathers. In the more static society envisaged by Confucius, roles would be well-defined, and while they might change, they would not do so violently. Many of Shihuang's inscriptions adhere to this principle, his very first one stating:

High and low are set apart,
Men and women observe their proper etiquette,
And fulfil their respective tasks.
The distinction is clear between public and private,
And peace reigns.

The final Confucian principle is that of "propriety," sometimes rendered as "ritual behaviour," "etiquette," or "civility." And it was his preoccupation with this virtue which led to the later charges that he was a pompous windbag and that the elaborate rites he demanded for weddings and funerals were wasteful and impractical. But none of these criticisms would have fazed Confucius, for he was convinced that even the smallest act of courtesy mirrored and expanded a righteous and humane mind. More importantly, Confucius saw the past as a better and more genteel time, an idyllic period when "the world was shared by all alike." By preserving and replicating the old forms of ritual and etiquette, he hoped that a better world would be restored. It was this love of history, the need to learn from it, that clashed most profoundly with Shihuang's desire to be first, to be unfettered by precedent, and one of the reasons he burned the books.

Confucius preached that the end result of "learning and practice" would be the creation of a different type of human being, the Confucian "gentleman," or more accurately, the "princely man." Only to men like these, would the government of the state be entrusted.

Although the *Analects* do not define the princely man, many passages, however, present a composite picture of a human being who was wise, brave and without anxiety, who practiced what he preached before preaching it, who concerned himself with the "Way" and not with profit, and who calmly and easily bore his mantle of humanity, "reaching below" to the masses to aid them in their quest to also become "princely men."

Finally, at the top of the pyramid, would rule the most princely of these men, the king who gained his position, not by heredity or force, but simply by his manifest virtue. And if this were the case, if the ruler were truly upright, "all would go well without orders" and "the people would become good." The True Ruler transforms by virtuous example, Confucius taught and he was once very explicit in conversation with the oligarch of his own state: *"Why, sir, should you employ capital punishment in your government? Just so long as you yourself desire the good, the people will be good. The virtue of the princely man may be compared to the wind and that of the commoners to the weeds. When the wind blows, the weeds cannot but bend!"*

This, then, was the advice which Confucius offered to the rulers of his time – the hard-headed princes who dealt constantly with spies, assassins, unruly and often disloyal subjects, the intrigues of their own families, and the ever-present threat of some rival state's army sweeping into their territory. Many of the rulers who sent him on his way must have echoed the sentiments of one who sighed that Confucius' words constituted but "a difficult and distant ideal."

Shihuang was not the first to reject the Confucian view of the ideal ruler, but when he did, it was not with a sigh.

The insignia on the robes of later officials indicated their rank in the hierarchical world envisioned by Confucius. This hanging scroll painting shows a Qing dynasty official in his robes of office.

Competing Systems of Thought in China

IN HIS OWN TIME, Confucius was but one of many itinerant scholars who travelled from state to state, and many were more successful than he. For example, Sun Zi, the reputed author of *The Art of War*, made his reputation as an advisor to the ruler of a rival state. The skeptical ruler asked him to demonstrate the efficacy of his techniques by training his 180 concubines to fight. Sun trained and armed them, but when it came time to demonstrate their prowess to the duke, they broke down in laughter. Sun demanded the right to execute the two "generals," the two favourite concubines of the duke, and despite the duke's protests, did just that. Due to his practical advice, he became an honoured and successful general, and his "thirteen chapters," have remained a manual for the Chinese military down to the present time.

Mo Zi, a near contemporary of Confucius, was far more successful in gaining the ear of the rulers than Confucius had been. It was not because of his doctrines, but because he and his band of disciples were experts in the art of defensive warfare, often rushing to threatened cities to advise on the handling of sieges. On one occasion, they are said to have arrived naked after a ten-day march during which they tore their clothing into shreds to wrap their bleeding feet!

On the whole, Mo Zi's message was anti-Confucian, recognizing that education, the prerequisite of the "princely man" could never be open to the peasantry. His doctrine also condemned the waste of costly ceremonials, and the irrelevance of poetry and music at a time when the drums of war sounded every day. There was a strain of idealism in Mo Zi's own philosophy, with its absolute condemnation of offensive war as the most wasteful of all human activity and his curiously modern belief that the reduction of government expenditure would generalize prosperity. And more than this, in his doctrine of "universal" or "overflowing" love, he even exceeded Christ's injunction to "Love they neighbour as thyself." Instead, he advocated total altruism – that one be "willing to destroy oneself from head to foot" for the sake of one's neighbour.

But where Mo Zi surpassed Confucius in his understanding of human psychology is that his philosophy contained incentives. For Confucius, goodness is its own reward, and for someone trying to change human behaviour, that is the central weakness in his teachings. He promised neither the riches of the world nor salvation in another world for those who were virtuous.

Mo Zi, in contrast, advanced the notion of "benefit" or "profit" as the mainspring of human action, and he promised that if Heaven, which desired the greatest good for all human beings, were honoured, the whole world, and everyone in it would prosper. He saw the ghosts and spirits which populated the world in his immensely superstitious age, as the messengers of Heaven. Confucius had advised that they "be kept at arm's length," but Mo Zi believed they should be heeded.

Mo Zi's "common man" approach touched a chord at all social levels, and his adherents easily outstripped those of Confucius for some centuries. Even Shihuang, in all his majesty, and with all the so-called "rational" scholars who surrounded him, was never to lose his awe of the spirits Mo Zi taught were messengers of great importance.

This representation of the forces of yin and yang is called the taiji *or the Supreme Ultimate. It explains the workings of the universe.*

▷ *Harem women were more likely to spend their time arranging flowers than fighting as Sun Zi insisted they do.*

Taoism and its Influence on Shihuang

ALONG WITH THE TEACHINGS of Confucius and Mo Zi, there were also many other schools of thought in ancient China. One was concerned with the complementary forces of Yin and Yang, and with the use of these forces to predict and manipulate the future. Another school debated abstract questions – the nature of space, time, quality, and reality, much in the fashion of their contemporary Greek analogues. And one, destined to be far more influential than the Mo-ists in China, debated the nature of "The Way."

Taoism was destined to have an immense influence on Qin Shihuang, though not in the manner one might expect.

In its original formulation, Taoism was the philosophy of Nature, of spontaneity and acceptance, of transcendence over the mundane; and a philosophy which advised any would-be ruler that the best government was no government – "a government whose name only is known to the people." This was *laissez-faire* at its best, and because it also advised that the practice of rule was simple, it was appealing. *"A sage rules his people thus: he empties their minds while filling their bellies. And while weakening their ambition, he strengthens their bones. He works to keep them innocent of knowledge and [excessive] desires, and keeps the educated ones from interference."*

These are the words of the philosopher Lao Zi, who may or may not have existed, and whose "5000-word classic" was produced, it is said, only under duress. Despairing at the state of his country, he was, so the story goes, forced by the Keeper of the Passes to write down his thoughts for posterity before he left (to become the Buddha, according to another legend).

Unlike so many of his contemporaries, Lao Zi did not travel the land seeking a ruler to implement his message. For him and his many followers, the ideal life was that of the recluse or hermit, alone in the wilderness, communing with the eternal mystery of the Tao, becoming one with Nature. Indeed, his most famous disciple, the philosopher Zhuang Zi (b. ca. 369 B.C.), was once approached by two officials of the great southern state of Chu whose ruler wished to make him his chief minister. Zhuang Zi, typically holding his fishing pole, is recorded to have said:

"I have heard that the state of Chu possesses a sacred tortoise, three-thousand-years-old, and that the king keeps it wrapped up and stores it in a box in his ancestral temple. Is this tortoise better off dead, its bones venerated, or would it be happier with its tail dragging in the mud?" And when the two ministers replied that it would be better off dragging its tail in the mud, Zhuang Zi told them to go away, for he too, would drag his tail in the mud.

The core of the Taoist message was non-interference, or non-action as expressed in Lao Zi's injunction *wei-wu-wei*, "do nothing and nothing will not be done." For believers of this philosophy, history was little more than the dreary story of man's interference with the Tao, and hence they opposed education, taxation, law and any other government function which might interfere with man's self-actualization. The Taoist writings were romantic and mystical, and if their tenets on government did not appeal to Shihuang, there was a side of their philosophy that did.

Zhuang Zi had written of "pure beings" and "perfected beings" who were able, after a lifetime of "non-seeking" the Tao, to pass through fire without being burned and to lie down in the snow without freezing – in short, to become immortal. In 212 B.C., when Shihuang began to construct the 270 palaces in which he would conceal himself from mortal eyes, he also changed the way he would refer to himself. Instead of using the royal "we," he would henceforth call himself the "Pure Being" (*zhenren*), employing the precise term used by Zhuang Zi. He was the only Chinese emperor ever to do so!

▷ *Laozi rides an ox on his journey to the west.*

Zhuang Zi was probably the wittiest, most romantic and most skeptical philosopher of the "Hundred Schools." Living towards the end of the Warring States period, he saw little hope for a world gone mad, and insisted on the cultivation of the individual, and the preservation of one's own life. He strongly believed that since knowledge was limitless and man's life limited, it was foolish and dangerous to pursue "the limitless with what was limited". This view is expressed in what is perhaps the most famous passage in his work. Zhuang Zi fell asleep and dreamed that he was a butterfly, fluttering about and enjoying himself. When he was suddenly awakened, he did not know whether he was Zhuang Zi dreaming he was a butterfly or a butterfly dreaming that he was Zhuang Zi! To him human life was a "Great Dream."

Mencius and Xun Zi

IN THE YEARS FOLLOWING the death of Confucius, the philosophers debated among themselves, sometimes elaborating and expanding the words of their masters, and sometimes even challenging them. The two most prominent of Confucius' disciples, for example, upheld most of his tenets, but were at odds with the Master on some points, and were diametrically opposed to each other on some fundamental questions. Mencius (ca. 372-289 B.C.) contended that human beings were born good, and needed only education and virtuous example from above to return, after the corrupting influence of a disordered world, to their "original hearts." He saw "the people," not the ruler, as the most essential element of the state, and his philosophy gave them something akin to the right of rebellion if Heaven warned a bad ruler to change his ways and he failed to respond. It was these "heavenly warnings" in the form of omens and portents – comets and meteors, earthquakes, floods and prophetic sayings – which came to obsess Shihuang in the last years of his life. Mencius' answer for any ruler who was so warned, was to advise the king to show compassion and love for his people, and thus rejuvenate and solidify his position. But Shihuang, whose huge conscriptions of labour made his people unhappy, did not take Mencius' advice. In the end, his own visions were too important to him and he would not give them up.

Xun Zi (fl. 298-238 B.C.) was also a Confucian, but a far more rationalistic one than Mencius. "Heaven operates with constant regularity," he said, denying that bad government brought about natural calamity. More importantly, he was convinced that human nature was evil, that all of us are born with a desire for gain, are greedy, envious and with "passions of the ear and eye." In his view, all human beings were in need of regulation, but in the societal hierarchy, the forms of regulation differed. For the "princely men," the rules of propriety and decorum were sufficient, but for the vast majority, only strict law and heavy punishment would work. Unlike Confucius, he was no foe of capital punishment!

And in those dying days of the old order, Xun Zi saw Qin snuff out the royal house of Zhou, and win victory after victory. He visited Qin in about 264 B.C., and was much impressed with what he saw. The people were disciplined and strong, the officials conscientious. But he also saw a darker side, and in the same passage remarked on how the Qin rulers "used their people harshly, frightened them with their power, cajoled them with rewards, and used punishments to force them to submit." He saw neither ritual, nor propriety, in Qin.

Nonetheless, it was because of his teachings, more than the work of any other philosopher, that the victory of Qin came about.

Mencius

The philosopher Mencius, who studied under the grandson of Confucius, followed most of his tenets, but placed a greater emphasis on the concept of "responsibility," which was perhaps instilled into him by his mother, one of China's most famous mothers. She moved her household three times so that young Mencius would be raised in the proper scholarly atmosphere, and on one occasion, when her son neglected his studies, destroyed her beautiful weaving in front of him to demonstrate that he was wasting his opportunities. On another occasion, when Mencius entered his bedroom to find his wife undressed, she was so ashamed that she asked him to divorce her. He was ready to do so, until his mother instructed him that he, too, was at fault for failing to knock before entering. He retained his wife.

Xun Zi, who probably died in 238 B.C., just as Shihuang attained his majority, is sometimes called a "left-handed" Confucian because of his rejection of some of the Master's teachings, particularly the views that law and punishment were unnecessary under a virtuous ruler, and that man learned from history. "The beginning of Heaven and earth," he proclaimed, "is today!"

Very much a rationalist, he also said that he hated the corruption of the governments of his time, the decadent states and the bad rulers who did not follow the Way but devoted themselves to magic and prayers, and to omens and portents. Although impressed with the Qin government when he visited the state, he lamented the lack of Confucian scholars and Confucian teaching there.

It was painstaking labour creating Chinese silk embroideries, as is shown in this detail from a Qing Dynasty woman's robe.

For the mother of Mencius, the unravelling of her handiwork was a severe object lesson to her son.

The Legalist Solution

IT IS OFTEN SAID that Xun Zi had two famous students, Han Feizi and Li Si. It would be more accurate to say that he had three famous students, for it was from these two men that Qin Shihuang learned his philosophy. From them, he learned that man was by nature evil, and that harsh law was the most effective regulator of human behaviour. These were Legalist tenets.

The philosophy which we term Legalism, or sometimes "legism" or statism," was the last of the "Hundred Schools" to develop a coherent theoretical position. This is not surprising, given that the great names in its development were practicing politicians like Shang Yang, who, concerned with the day-to-day details of state management, had neither the time nor the inclination for what they regarded as idle speculation. In fact, Han Feizi (d. 233 B.C.), the synthesizer of Legalism, regarded the speculations of the Hundred Schools not only as idle, but as dangerous. "While stupid and deceptive teachings and heretical and contradictory talk ... are listened to equally, how can there be anything but chaos?"

For the Legalists, all morality was tied to the state which was the highest good, and anything done to preserve, strengthen and expand it was, by definition, good. To achieve their statist aims the Legalists used three principles – supreme power vested in an absolute ruler, subtle techniques of statecraft to manipulate officials, and harsh, detailed law applied regularly and without distinction to everyone below the ruler. These principles, of course, grew from Xun Zi's conviction that human beings were by nature evil and in need of regulation by law. But his three students took these principles much further than he would have ever imagined.

They believed the position of the ruler, his status and authority, had to be beyond challenge, if the regicides and usurpations so common in the period were to cease. And the first step in this process was the elevation of the ruler to that of a mysterious and god-like figure, for as an early theorist put it: "A flying dragon rides on the clouds and a soaring serpent strolls through the mist. When the clouds disperse and the mists clear away, dragon and serpent are then no different than earthworms and ants."

Shihuang took this advice to heart, hiding himself away so effectively in his 270 palaces, "that no one knew his whereabouts."

And there were other ways of raising the dignity of the throne, all of them outlined in Han Feizi's works, and indeed, demonstrated in the lives of Li Si and Shihuang.

The best ruler would brook no criticism, nor would he accept advice unless it had been specifically requested. Han Feizi praises an ancestor of Shihuang who was informed by his chief minister that the tutors of his son were corrupting the boy with Confucian doctrine. The minister recommended the death penalty for the tutors. They were executed, but, so too was the informer for daring to recommend a course of action to the ruler!

Ordinary human ethics had no place in politics, and the ruler did not "transform by example," as Confucius would have it, but by swift, stern action against which there was no appeal. Han Feizi also praised the actions of a Duke of Qi who executed two Taoist recluses who could be neither "encouraged or intimidated" into his service. In Legalist theory, the ruler should be able to command instant obedience from all those below him, and on more than one occasion, Shihuang's servitors, aware of the danger involved, decided to flee rather than attempt to resign from their duties under him.

Standardization was an important feature of Legalist philosophy. This bronze weight is hollow and is inscribed with two long decrees relating to the standardization of measures.

芒種時己屆齡
暖麥歡涼未經
水土氣趣候插
釋秧御步復伸
手鬆直分科行
不獨其袋牀服
睛敝或去

In Legalist theory, agriculture was the essential occupation for the Blackhaired people.

The Tutor of Shihuang

AS HAN FEIZI TAUGHT, "The enlightened ruler does not govern his people, but rather his officials." In Legalist theory it was the officials who constituted the greatest threat to the ruler and his position, and Feizi offered certain techniques by which a ruler could bring them under control. He devoted much thought to this problem, and in the thirtieth chapter of his work he summarizes his findings in the "seven methods" so often compared to the work of the sixteenth-century statesman, Nicolo Machiavelli.

Fezi, however, is more explicit than the Italian statesman, advising that the enlightened ruler should:

1) know and compare all the various possibilities;
2) punish failure with unvarying severity to maintain the awe in which he is held;
3) grant generous and reliable rewards for success;
4) listen to all views, and hold the proposer responsible for every word;
5) issue unfathomable orders and make deceptive assignments;
6) conceal one's own knowledge when making enquiries of a minister;
7) speak in opposites and act in contraries.

These were lessons which Shihuang learned well. No minister ever succeeded in dominating him and those who see Li Si as a "guiding genius" are probably mistaken.

Han Fezi also said: "All the great matters of the ruler of men are either matters of law or methods. The laws are to be compiled in documents, stored in every government office and made known to all the people."

The 1975 discovery of a number of bamboo slips of Qin law in the coffin of one of Shihuang's officials who died in 217 B.C., shows how seriously the law was taken, for it was even to accompany this magistrate to the afterlife! The rule of law was the fundamental principle of Legalist philosophy, and as scholars examine these finds, it becomes more and more apparent that in Qin, the laws were detailed, regular, and embodied both heavy punishments and large rewards.

The laws, however, had a particular purpose. Penal law and the system of rewards were seen by Shihuang and his advisors as the twin "handles" to be used by the ruler to manipulate his people for two purposes: war and agriculture.

In a very famous passage, called the "Five Vermin of the State," Han Feizi demonstrates a view unique in all of Chinese antiquity, and one to which Shihuang surely subscribed. In it he called for the elimination of five classes of people – men of learning, itinerant scholars like Confucius, mercenary soldiers, nobles and courtiers, and merchants and artisans. In short, he wished to expunge from the state all distractions such as learning, culture and mercantile activity, and create a nation of soldiers and farmers, rather in the mould of ancient Sparta.

This is the context – agriculture and war – into which we must put so many of Shihuang's activities. From the time he reached his majority in 238 B.C., his armies were not idle for a single year until the unification. Even after 221 B.C. he sent his troops against the Xiongnu in the north and the aboriginal peoples of the south. Warfare against external enemies united his people and made them docile, amenable to his decrees. And as he opened new lands and colonized them, he sent not only experienced agriculturists, but merchants, incompetent officials, and even those among the young who had been slow to marry and establish their own farms. In Legalist theory, agriculture was the root occupation, the basis of any state's wealth, and Shihuang had not forgotten his training.

The Chinese historians who, in later centuries, wrote about Shihuang's Blackhaired people, portrayed them as a nation of dumb, militarized farmers.

The name of Han Feizi written in Chinese.

As advised by the philosopher Han Feizi, severe punishments for failure were part of Chinese life under Shihuang.

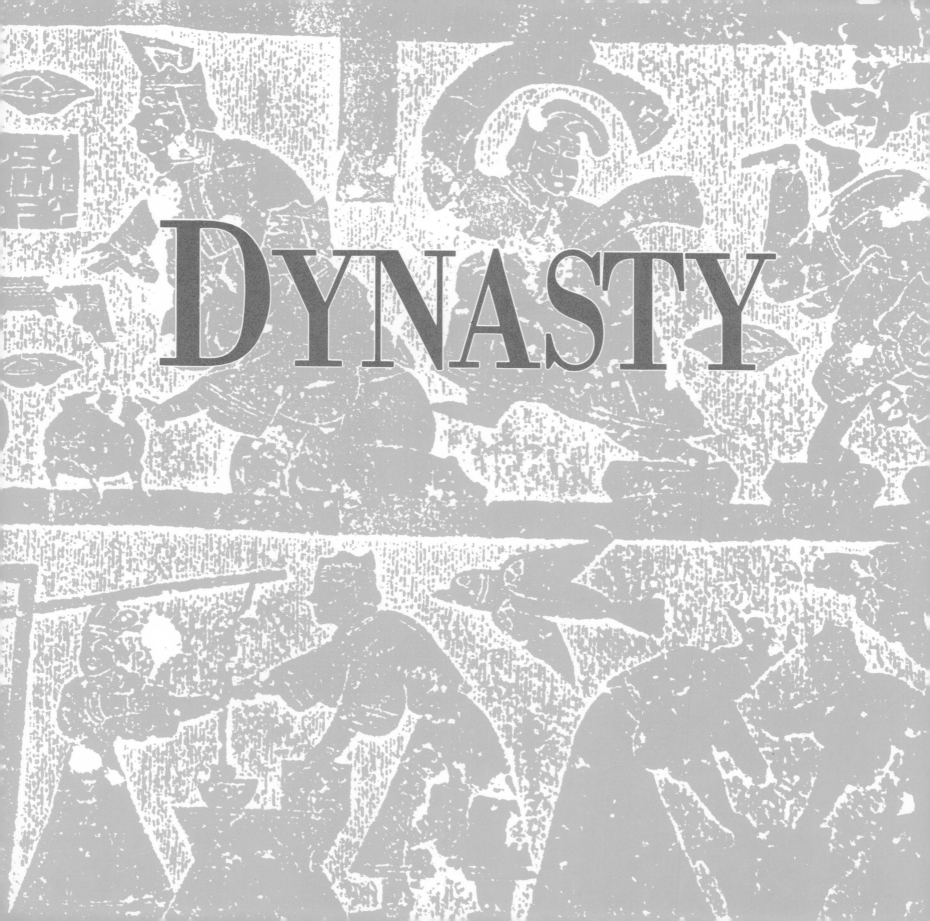

THE EMPEROR AND HIS BLACKHAIRED PEOPLE

Life in the Qin Dynasty

Qin Law

THE MOST PERSISTENT STEREOTYPE of the Qin Dynasty, and one that has endured for over 2,000 years is that it was a wholly "Legalist" regime with every aspect of life controlled by laws for which harsh, cruel and disproportionate punishments were meted out when they were broken. This view arose because of the writings by Qin's earliest critics and also because of the failure of contemporary statesmen such as Shang Yang and Han Feizi to write down the specific details of the Qin law.

In 1975, however, in a tomb near present-day Wuhan, over 1100 bamboo strips of Qin law were discovered. Dating back to 217 B.C., four years after Shihuang established his dynasty, they had been buried with a local magistrate, and dealt with both penal and civil law. Rather narrow in scope, they probably represent a guide for the type of decisions he would have to make in his official career. They are mostly concerned with the management of granaries, labour by both free conscripts and convicts, and the kinds of criminal cases a typical magistrate of the period would be called upon to investigate. However, incomplete as they are, they throw new light on the laws of Shihuang and many long-held views must now be revised.

There is no doubt that the punishments for the more serious crimes could be harsh, and the usual punishment was beheading. But cruel as that penalty may have been, there were two others which were considered far more degrading. One, translated as "being torn apart by chariots," may simply have meant the public exposure of the corpse; and the other consisted of being cut in two at the waist. These penalties often incorporated the principle of joint responsibility in which a lighter punishment such as forced labour was imposed upon the criminal's family.

Physical punishments were a terrible disgrace for all concerned since they meant the mutilation of the human body which was considered something which must be kept inviolate as, according to the tenets of filial piety, it was a gift from one's parents. In later Chinese law, strangulation or hanging were both seen as a privileged form of capital punishment because they did not desecrate the body. During the Qin Dynasty, these capital punishments must have been reserved for such serious crimes as treason and murder, and it is of some interest to note that nowhere in the discovered documents is there any mention of live burial. This throws some doubt on the account of Shihuang's "burial of the scholars" in 212 B.C.

As a penalty, forced labour was far more common than these capital punishments and was applied to a wide variety of crimes. The condemned were usually sent to work on construction projects such as the Great Wall. This punishment usually involved some form of mutilation, as well, the most severe being the amputation of both feet. In other cases, the nose was cut off or the criminal was tattooed on the forehead or cheeks, and in every case, the Wall builders had their hair and beards shaved off. It seems likely that female convicts also suffered some form of mutilation before being transported to cook for the male labourers. Thus all criminals displayed the mark of their shame.

Other sentences of forced labour included such things as agricultural work, guard duty and service in government storehouses and workshops. This duty was for a specified period of time and was the penalty paid for such crimes as theft, the severity of punishment depending on the value of the stolen goods and the existence of extenuating factors. Banishment, and flogging with a bamboo pole were also frequently used as punishment, and though we are certain castration was common, we do not know which crimes warranted this penalty. Fines were also common, and applied most frequently to officials or to those holding honorary rank, but they could also be used to redeem more severe punishments.

Qin law was written on wooden slips such as these. Scholars are currently attempting to decipher examples found recently in a Qin tomb.

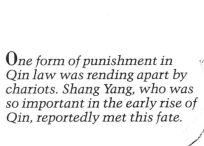

*O*ne form of punishment in Qin law was rending apart by chariots. Shang Yang, who was so important in the early rise of Qin, reportedly met this fate.

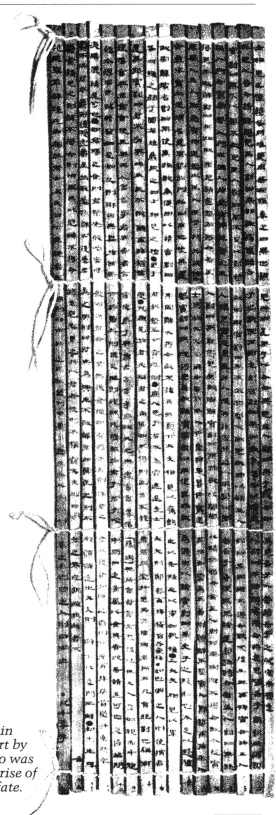

Eunuchs

CASTRATION SEEMS TO HAVE BEEN a common punishment in Qin law, and the most famous of those to suffer the penalty was a man called Zhao Gao. He was the man most responsible for the fall of Qin, and was the first of many eunuchs blamed by traditional historians for the fall of later dynasties.

According to his biography, his elder and younger brothers were also eunuchs. He, himself, had been condemned to castration for some serious crime by Meng I, the younger brother of the general, Meng Tian. Thus, he hated the family, and after the death of Shihuang, succeeded in having both brothers put to death.

Eunuchs had been an important part of the political structure since perhaps the eighth century B.C. when they are first mentioned in the texts. They had, however, existed long before that, probably as early as five or six hundred years before, when polygamy became part of the Chinese marriage structure.

In the earliest periods, it was captured enemies who were probably made into eunuchs, and for much of Chinese history, they came from the south where the aboriginal tribes were slow to be assimilated. Castration was also one of the Five Great Punishments even prior to Qin times and since the penalty was often coupled with a period of state slavery, eunuchs were employed for a variety of tasks, but they were most often placed in the harem of rulers and other high officials. Here they guarded and taught the women, and performed the heavy work of the palace without posing a threat to the purity of the royal blood-line. They also helped to educate the sons of concubines, and Zhao Gao, for instance, instructed Hu Hai, the Second Emperor, in the code of law. If one of their pupils gained the throne, their continued influence was assured and the eunuchs within the palace tended to work together, conspiring against the scholar-officials who had access to the emperors only in formal policy sessions. Eunuchs shared the emperor's most private moments, often escorting the favoured concubine to his bed, and were often privy to his most secret policy decisions.

No sources detail the method of castration in the Qin period but it was probably the same as in later ages when the entire genitalia were removed and a plug inserted, with the new eunuch forbidden to drink water for three days. Convalescence took three months and after that, palace duties began.

It was palace ladies like these who were often the closest associates of eunuchs.

Eunuchs were usually presented with the severed organs called their *bao* or "treasure." These had to be preserved and shown to the head eunuch to prove that they had truly been castrated if they wished to obtain promotion within the palace, and they were also kept for the eunuchs' burial. Eunuchs believed that if they were buried with their "treasure," they would be restored to masculinity in the next world.

The *Shiji* mentions a few cases of voluntary castration by ambitious men who "wished to be close to the ruler," but it does not seem to have been common in Shihuang's time. In later periods, those living under the crushing burden of poverty, sometimes castrated their sons and grandsons in the hope that they would enter the emperor's service and become influential enough to support the whole family. During the Ming Dynasty in the fifteenth century, voluntary castration became such a severe problem that it was forbidden by law, but

the dynastic records tell us that at the end of the dynasty there were 20,000 applicants for 3,000 positions in the palace. When the dynasty fell in 1644, there were over 100,000 eunuchs in the capital!

Traditional Chinese histories attribute the fall of three dynasties, the Han, Tang, and Ming primarily to the eunuchs' baleful influence on the government.

Eunuchs were especially important under female rulers. Pictured here is Ci Xi, the famed Empress Dowager, who held power for almost half a century until her death in 1908. With her are two of her favourite eunuchs.

Crime and Punishment

JUST AS IN OUR OWN society, murder, infanticide, and injuring a fellow citizen were considered serious crimes during Shihuang's reign. However, extenuating circumstances played a large part in determining the punishments to be meted out.

For instance, if a newly-born child were killed for economic reasons, the punishment was tattooing and a period of forced labour. If, however, the child had been born deformed, or "had strange things on its body," to do away with it was not considered a crime.

Immaturity was no excuse when it came to murder, however, and if a youth, someone not yet of full stature, was involved in a plot to kill someone, he was executed and his corpse was exposed to the populace.

Premeditation was the crucial condition when a person was accused of wounding or injuring another citizen. If the offense was committed with a needle or awl, or any ready-to-hand tool, the punishment was a fine of two suits of armour. If, however, the wound had been inflicted by a weapon which had to be drawn from a sheath, a much heavier penalty was enforced – tattooing and forced labour.

Family morality was also heavily regulated. A man who repudiated his wife and failed to report it in writing to the authorities was fined two suits of armour. And so was the divorced wife!

If children of the same mother but different fathers had sexual relations, they were both beheaded, a punishment reflecting the traditional Chinese horror of incest, and also suggesting that Shihuang's injunction against the remarriage of widows, in one of his inscriptions, was not honoured.

A wife who left her husband and married another man would be divorced by him if he discovered that she had been married previously. If not, he faced forced labour and so did she. And a man who found his wife in bed with another man was allowed to kill them both as long as he acted immediately. If he took the time to think it over and then slew them, he could be tried for murder.

Under Shihuang, China remained a firm and uncompromising patriarchy and although the attitudes towards women embodied in the laws of his time were not new, as part of his legacy, they continued on as part of the patriarchal code in the later dynasties.

Transported colonists faced a difficult existence in some of the more desolate parts of China.

The Magistrates of Qin

AS SHIHUANG RULED UNDER the principle that "the Emperor governs the officials and the officials govern the people," the officials' conduct was expected to set an example for the populace. The law, therefore, regulated many aspects of the officials' existence ranging from their uniforms to their deportment. For example, an official who had been seen carrying women in his official chariot was fined two suits of armour.

Above all else, the law required that officials carry out their duties with both competence and exactitude. In the granaries, not only was a precise annual accounting required but the weights and measures used were also subjected to an annual checkup by the central authorities. Since the grain was destined to be distributed both for official salaries as well as rations for the free labour conscripts, shortfalls resulted in heavy punishments for those responsible. Officials were also punished if their negligence had allowed rain or other inclement conditions to spoil the grain in their storehouses, and that went so far as to include rodents in the barns. On one inspection, three rat-holes were discovered, and the official in charge was fined one shield. Three mouse-holes, the law decreed, were the equivalent of one rat-hole!

In the eventuality that, despite the fine distinctions in the Qin code of law, something had not been covered, the principle of "analogy" was incorporated into the law. If, for example, a felon knocked out another man's teeth in a fight, and this crime was not included in the law, the magistrate could penalize the offender in the same way he would have if the man had inflicted "welts and bruises." This principle remained a feature of traditional Chinese law up to the twentieth century.

Qin magistrates also had to function as policemen or detectives. They were given models for the conduct of investigations in the form of either actual or hypothetical cases which ranged from a woman who miscarried because she was in a fight with another woman, to a man who had failed to report his leprosy. In each case the magistrate was advised on how he should proceed. One of the more intriguing cases concerns a man found hanged. Was it suicide or murder?

The document first outlines the report of the investigating magistrate. In almost photographic detail, it explains the disposition of the room, the state of the corpse, the length of the rope, the dead man's clothing, and the lack of such clues as sharp weapons or footprints near the body.

The text continues:

When investigating, it is essential first to carefully examine and consider the traces. One should go alone to the place where the corpse is, and consider the knot of the rope ... Then observe whether the tongue protrudes or not, how far the feet and head are distant from the place of the knot and the ground, and whether he had undischarged faeces and urine or not. Then untie the rope and observe whether the mouth and nose emit a sigh or not ... [After freeing the body, remove the clothes and] observe the body, from inside the hair on his head down to the perineum. ...

The magistrate was then alerted to the suspicious signs which may have indicated murder rather than suicide, and was instructed to question carefully all members of the man's household.

It appears that the magistrates during Shihuang's reign were required to be the Sherlock Holmes of their time.

"tiger"

Each Qin magistrate had his distinctive badge of office. This so-called mandarin square, although from a later period, follows the tradition of identifying rank by insignia on the robes.

The embroidered tiger square represents a rank in the military hierarchy.

A Net of Responsibility

IT IS CLEAR THAT SHIHUANG expected more than just competence from his officials – he demanded excellence, and law after law bears this out. For instance, when a wall was built, the men in charge were responsible for their work for a full year after the job was completed. If, for any reason, the wall collapsed, the official in charge was held criminally liable!

Officials in charge of the royal hunts were fined either a suit of armour or a shield if the quarry – a tiger or leopard – escaped. If the horses drawing the ruler's chariot were injured during the hunt, there were also penalties. "A tear in the skin is fined one shield; for two inches, the fine is to be two shields. For over two inches the fine is two suits of armour." We do not know exactly what a shield or suit of armour was worth, but we do know that in Qin times, the reward for denouncing a murderer, thief or absconded convict was two ounces of gold, the equivalent of 1250 copper cash. A suit of armour may have been worth about the same.

Qin Shihuang's laws for his bureaucrats also included a regulation which may make modern readers envious. "When forwarding royal commands, as well as documents marked 'urgent,' these are to be forwarded immediately. Those that are not urgent are to be dealt with in one day..."

There were also laws regulating the daily rations and treatment of conscripted labourers who could not be kept too long on the job or forced to perform unreasonable labour. These laws do not seen too harsh and the greatest hardship for these men was probably to work far away from their families in unhealthy and dangerous parts of the land.

Even some sound ecological principals were embodied in Qin law:

... In the second month of spring, one should not venture to cut timber in the forests or block water courses. Except in the months of summer, one should not venture to burn weeds to make ashes, to collect young animals, eggs or fledglings. One should not ... poison fish or tortoises or arrange pitfalls and nets. By the seventh month these prohibitions are lifted ... In the season of young animals, one should not venture to take dogs to go hunting..."

Reflecting the cosmological principles which preceded his reign, Shihuang's laws viewed men and women as part of the cosmos, and their behaviour was supposed to adapt to the

rhythms of the wider world and so produce harmony. The presumption for criminals, or even those denounced as criminals, was not "innocent until proven guilty," but the opposite. Torture was permitted in Qin jails to extract confessions, but these confessions were regarded with suspicion and there was a right of appeal against some judgements.

So detailed were the Qin laws, that the judges obviously had to know their jobs, and, at least on paper, the laws were fairly administered. They had been written with care, and the judicial precepts were centuries old, probably going back to the eighth century. Any irregularities on the part of the magistrates were punished.

All in all, the laws of Shihuang seem strict rather than unduly harsh. But it must have been difficult for the ordinary man to know all their intricacies, and many were undoubtedly caught in the network of laws they did not fully understand.

The historians who see the harsh laws as the root of the Qin Dynasty's fall, really mean that there were too many laws, and, as a result, too many convictions of people who had unwittingly broken them. To these people, their punishment would have been unjust, and many of them finally rebelled.

The notorious severity of Qin law is illustrated in the passage written in the calligraphic style of Qin times.

Qin law was concerned with the balance of nature. It offered protection to birds, animals, fish and even to trees. Wood could be cut out of season only to build a coffin for one's deceased parent.

The Imperial Tours

ONCE HIS BASIC LEGAL SYSTEM was in place, Shihuang began a "hands-on" inspection of his vast new domain through a series of tours that were remarkable in their scope.

In the past, with only a few exceptions, the rulers of China had preferred to remain safely in their palaces, "facing the south," and relying on reports from officials to assess the state of the nation.

Shihuang was different. He made five imperial inspection tours during a single decade of his reign and the last extended for almost a full year.

His tours were not made solely for religious or strategic purposes. He also travelled to see what he had wrought, to awe his subjects with his might, to record his achievements, and to learn more about his people and his country.

The costs were enormous, of course. The local communities had to provision the expeditions and billet the hundreds and thousands of retainers who travelled with the emperor. But Shihuang was above all these mundane details, travelling by royal prerogative and seeking for immortality.

His first tour, in 220 B.C., was the only one which took him to the west – back to the heartland of his heritage, to the southern part of present-day Kansu province where his ancestors had begun their march so long before.

On this tour, he did not erect a monument. But on his return, he began to build a palace complex in Xianyang centred around

his former ancestral temples. It was to be called the "Pivot of Heaven" and is known today as the Afang Palace. And he ordered it connected by a covered walkway to Mount Li where he selected a site for his own tomb.

Thus, Shihuang placed himself firmly into the context of his own history.

His next four tours took him to the east, to the mountains, long regarded as sacred, and to the sea.

The second tour, in 219 B.C., turned into a pilgrimage, when he stopped in the ancient state of Lu – the birthplace of Confucius and the home of the most respected ritualists in the land. Here he discussed with them the proper form of "the sacrifices to Heaven and earth and to the mountains and the rivers." And then, secure in his knowledge, he ascended Mount Tai, the holiest of all China's mountains to perform what later became the most awe-inspiring of all imperial rites – the *feng* and *shan* sacrifices.

In all of Chinese history, only five of the more than 200 emperors who followed Shihuang have felt themselves worthy to carry out this most solemn ceremony. The aim of the sacrifice was twofold: the acknowledgment of a Heavenly Mandate to rule and a report to Heaven of complete success in that task.

Qin Shihuang travelled with a huge entourage on his tours of inspection.

Food and Drink in the Qin Empire

ALTHOUGH WE DO NOT KNOW specifically what Shihuang ate or drank, from a variety of sources, we can gather some idea of the cuisine of the period.

In northern China, the principal grain was millet, but other cereal grains like wheat, hemp and barley were common. Soybeans were grown in China, probably before they appeared anywhere else in the world, perhaps as early as the first millenium, and one pre-Qin text, the *Book of Odes*, lists no fewer than forty-six different vegetables in its poems. For meat dishes, the dog and the pig have the longest history in China, but cattle, sheep and goats were also eaten during the time of Shihuang. Chicken, goose, pheasant and quail were the common fowl, and we even hear of the consumption of vultures! Carp, turtles, frogs and snails were also a common feature in the kitchens of the land-locked state of Qin. There were at least four distinct kinds of alcoholic beverage and we know that drinking parties were common at that time.

The cooking methods were highly sophisticated – ingredients had to be properly proportioned, the time and temperature for each ingredient carefully measured, and the most important property of any dish was considered to be the mixing of flavours. Some of the cooking methods were a result of the care lavished on individual dishes for sacrificial offerings, and some of the richness of Chinese cuisine developed because of the interest Shihuang and his successors took in the quest for immortality. Certain roots and herbs found today on the menu of every Chinese restaurant were initially ingested to obtain long life, and the Eastern Isles of the Immortals were said to produce certain fungi, most importantly the *linggi* or "divine" mushroom which guaranteed it.

The following dishes are mentioned in poems from Shihuang's period:
– ribs of fatted ox
– stewed turtle and roast kid with yam sauce
– goose cooked in sour sauce
– flesh of the great crane
– seethed tortoise
– fried honey-cakes of rice flour and malt-sugar sweetmeats
– plump orioles, pigeons and geese flavoured with broth of jackal's meat
– dog cooked in bitter herbs and zingiber-flavoured mince
– salad of artemisia with stewed magpie and green goose.

A work, *(Liji)*, which probably appeared shortly after the fall of the Qin speaks of:
– pheasant-soup made with snail-juice and water-squash
– boneless meat sauce mixed with mouldy millet and kept for a hundred days before serving.

The same work also gives us some recipes for foods which were served to the elderly and to the upper classes. These recipes, which insist on such ingredients as "rice grown on dry soil," suggest that the preparation was painstaking for many dishes. For example, a suckling pig was stuffed with dates, baked in clay, and the crackling was then mixed with seasonings and smeared over the pig which was then deep-fried. But this was

This beautifully decorated bronze vessel, called a dui, *can be separated to form two serving bowls.*

not the end of the recipe. Next it was sliced and the slices were boiled in "fragrant herbs" and water for three days and nights. The final result was served with pickled meat and vinegar.

The cooking and eating vessels during Shihuang's time were made of bronze or pottery, and the type of food served in each was subject to regulation, so that food or drink made from grain was restricted to bronze vessels. And certainly within the palace, the meals were served with a ritual so exacting that when a fish was placed on a plate, its position was determined by the season of the year!

A tomb discovered in 1972 and dating from about 168 B.C. contained no fewer than twenty-four different meats and fish, and we may be sure that with the resources of the whole empire at his disposal, Shihuang enjoyed a diet every bit as varied!

Beautifully decorated and highly valued, lacquer plates like this graced the tables of Shihuang's feasts. Lacquer is both durable and versatile, able to withstand heat and impervious to liquids. Archaeologists have found many examples of lacquer which are more than 2,000 years old.

The Artifacts of the Qin Dynasty

IN ADDITION TO THE GREAT mausoleum of Qin Shihuang, more than six hundred Qin tombs have been excavated, spanning the long history of the state from about the eighth century B.C. to the end of the Qin dynasty. From these discoveries, it is clear that from the beginning, Qin was a state with highly individualistic characteristics. People were buried, for instance, in a distinctive posture, with the lower limbs stretched up, rather than laid out flat. The interior of some of the large tombs are coated with charcoal and green lime-clay, and this is probably the earliest use of these materials to seal tombs. Human sacrifice was common in the tombs of Shihuang's ancestors, so it is perhaps not surprising that his "childless concubines" were forced to accompany him into his mausoleum.

In these newly-discovered tombs, a rich store of artifacts contributes to further knowledge about life in the state of Qin, both before and after the unification.

We find, for instance, examples of the standardized weights and measures of the dynasty, some of them inscribed with words of praise for Shihuang's accomplishments and injunctions to the officials who used them to make sure that the Blackhaired people would understand the nature of the emperor's reforms. There are also measuring cups designed so that prisoners and conscripts received precisely the amount of daily rations to which they were entitled by law. Some of these vessels were inscribed with Shihuang's edicts as a tangible reminder of his power both to his officials and to his victims.

Bronze bells have also been found, the most recent a fine example from the area of Shihuang's mausoleum, which reminds us that in Shihuang's program of standardization, even music was included. His court musicians are said to have tuned their bells to musical stones, and then to have standardized all the bells in China to the same pitches. Highly-ornamented, the Qin bells were so perfectly crafted that when hung in a frame and struck from the outside, they could play complex melodies.

At the time of Shihuang, Chinese musical instruments were not classified by the way they were played, but by the eight materials from which they were made. At the court of the emperor there were instruments of gourd, bamboo, wood, silk, clay, metal, stone and skin. Each was associated with a season and with some aspect of nature, so that the bamboo pipes, for instance, were associated with spring and mountains, while bells were associated with autumn and the phenomenon of dampness. Bells were also associated with the west, the Qin homeland, and this made them particularly appropriate for use in the dynasty. Stone drums were associated with the

This pottery figure was discovered near Shihuang's tomb.

northwest, so they too, were an important part both of the ritual and of the enjoyment of music. Stone "drums" with inscriptions cursing the state of Chu, Qin's arch-enemy, have been found, and they were probably used in rituals before battles with Chu.

During Shihuang's "burning of the books," musical manuscripts were not spared, and a work attributed to Confucius, *The Classic of Music*, appears to have been destroyed, one of the major losses to future civilizations.

Archaeology in China has but scratched the surface of the Qin remains, and there is no doubt that someday we will have a much fuller picture of the dynasty than we have at present.

⇕ **M**any of the Qin pottery measures were inscribed using seals. Each seal consisted of 4 characters and formed an edict by Shihuang relating to unification.

This pottery vessel was the most common type of liquid container in Qin.

The Search for Immortality

IT IS INTERESTING TO SPECULATE upon why Shihuang was the first ruler to climb Mount Tai for his ritual sacrifices. Perhaps it was his ego that demanded it or perhaps it was his sense of style. Shihuang obviously knew that Mount Tai, with its point of highest elevation, was the place where spirits from above descended to the world below. To pass such a sacred place without acknowledgment of the presence of the gods was to invite their wrath. The Chinese believed in sacred mountains as cosmic axes and the points of the creation of the world. In Shihuang's time, five peaks were considered sacred, and Mount Tai was paramount.

Convinced of his own oneness with heaven and earth, Shihuang descended from Mount Tai after his sacrifice and took shelter from a rainstorm under a great tree. When the storm passed, it is written that he rewarded the tree with the title of Minister of the Fifth Rank.

He also left a stone monument on Mount Tai praising his achievements of unification and pacification and announced that "All under Heaven" now had one law and one form. And he reminded his subjects that his tours to faroff places were for their benefit, and that he was tireless in his care for them, rising "at the first light of dawn" and lying down to sleep "only in the dead of night."

After Mount Tai, Shihuang proceeded regally to the beautiful terraced lands of Langyai on the eastern coast where he viewed the sea, the Eastern extremity of his realm, and looked towards the Islands of Penglai, the fabled home of the Immortals.

Shihuang was so captivated with this lovely land that he remained there for three months and built a grand tower which he adorned with the longest of his inscriptions. He also ordered 30,000 families from other parts of the empire to settle there, and exempted them from taxation and conscription for twelve years, the better to colonize the land.

He finally returned to his capital by a circuitous route and along the way met a group of magicians who begged for permission to mount an expedition to the fairy islands of Penglai to find the elixir of immortality. Delighted with the idea, Shihuang sent the magicians out with a conscripted force of "thousands of youths and maidens" to find the mysterious potion.

To the best of our knowledge, they never returned.

If, as the legends said, the islands were lands of milk and honey, "where all creatures, the birds and the beasts, were white and the gates and palaces were fashioned of gold and silver," it is understandable why this expedition decided to remain. Legend also has it that the comely youths sent on this expedition were the founders of the Japanese race.

A depiction of the land of the immortals, sought by Shihuang throughout his life.

The Beliefs of Shihuang

THE QIN DYNASTY has always been regarded as the supreme embodiment of Legalism in action. And Shihuang, as its head, has always been seen by later historians, Confucians to a man, as a single-minded devotee of that philosophy. In their one-dimensional view, he was a tyrant and a tiger, a maker of draconian law, and a destroyer of all competing systems of thought. In this case, however, history is wrong.

Shihuang may have been many of the things he was accused of by the historians, but stupid he was not. He had at his disposal the finest minds of his age, his seventy "scholars of wide learning" and his three hundred observers of the Heavens. His biography shows that he consulted them on a wide variety of matters, all the way from the interpretation of his dreams to the question of abolishing feudalism. And the very fact that these advisors possessed such a wide range of expertise makes clear the eclectic nature of thought in his time. The labels "Confucian" and "Legalist" are little more than helpful conventions, and in many cases, they mislead us rather than inform.

If we really want to understand the emperor's beliefs, we should look at his actions. No one would deny that his laws and his armies, his book-burning and his forced labour conscriptions were more closely identified with Legalism than with any other system of thought. But what, then, are we to make of his inscriptions, filled as they are with "Confucian" sentiments – "He cares for the common people," "The common people know peace," "All people benefit from his benevolence," and "He overcame all the other states by virtue"? And what are we to make of his constant quest for immortality, a concept so closely identified with Taoism?

What emerges most clearly from these seeming contradictions is that like most brilliant men, Shihuang was adaptable, able to select and fashion for his own use the philosophies of the time. For ruling the state, he selected Legalism with its emphasis on strength, discipline and organization. For ruling his Blackhaired people, he chose Confucianism, with its emphasis on a humane ruler who cared for the common people. And for his personal spiritual satisfaction, the emperor turned to Taoism and the folk beliefs which had become a part of it.

During Shihuang's reign there was, as yet, no imperial religion. In later periods, and beginning with the Han dynasty, emperors would perform a large number of carefully defined rituals – an annual sacrifice to Heaven, the ceremonial plowing of the first furrow to inaugurate the agricultural season, the sacrifice of the Southern Suburb, ceremonials to honour their ancestors and sometimes to honour Confucius and other "sages." But these rituals were not possible until both the empire and culture had been unified and defined. During the short-lived Qin dynasty, imperial religion was still in the process of formation, and the local religious observances of the conquered states were far more prominent.

Although profoundly interested in both the sacred, and later, in the supernatural beliefs of his land, Shihuang fashioned his religion to suit his needs, and he performed numerous local rites which were no longer used as imperial ceremonials after his time. Before we accuse him of cynicism, however, we must remember that he had only two principal options in his religious observances. He could either convert the gods and ceremonials of the Qin state to empire-wide significance, and so stress his state's dominance, or he could discount Qin religion and create something new, something unique for a new empire. But he did neither, because for him, religion was too important and personal a matter to be dominated by political considerations. When it came to his own salvation, he left no stone unturned, trying to cover all his bets.

Shihuang constantly sought the advice of his seventy scholars of wide learning.

Mightier than the Gods

WHILE THE FRUITLESS quest for immortality was going on in the east, Shihuang returned to his capital, pausing at the Si River in Jiangsu where he was captivated again by another mystic tale.

This river was said to be the repository for the last of the nine sacred bronze tripods of Zhou. These huge vessels were said to have been fashioned in the dim past to represent each of the nine regions of China. Qin already possessed eight and to make perfect the legitimacy of the dynasty, the complete set was required.

Shihuang imperiously ordered one thousand divers to be brought from the countryside and sent them deep into the river to search for the tripod. The search was unsuccessful and artists in later years painted pictures of the divers battling huge monsters from the deep who had impeded their task.

This failure was regarded as heavenly disapproval of Shihuang's rule and the First Emperor was angry and deeply anxious. But there was another disturbing omen to follow.

While attempting to cross the mighty Yangtse River to return to the capital, Shihuang's boats were assailed by heavy winds and rain, and the emperor's vessel almost capsized. Shihuang was enraged. This was the last straw after the failure of both the quest for immortality and the search for the elusive ninth tripod.

He discovered that the guardian deity of that part of the river was the daughter of Yao, one of China's legendary sage-kings, and that she was buried under a nearby hill.

He then ordered a force of three thousand convicts to destroy all the trees and vegetation on the hill and paint it bright red – the bloody color worn by convicted criminals. It was an act of defiance, and showed clearly that Shihuang considered himself mightier than the gods of heaven and not subject to the rules that governed mere mortals.

Twice more, in 218 and 215 B.C., he travelled back to the east, back to his beloved mountains and to the sea where he was convinced that the secret of immortality was still to be found.

On the 218 B.C. inspection, he almost lost his life to an assassin, but few details are known other than the fact that the would-be killer was never caught.

On the following tour, its primary purpose, was once again to seek the herbs of immortality. He decided to destroy the fortifications of the area, to ensure that it remained peaceful, and again sent out his magicians. Once more there was failure, and frustrated, Shihuang, returned to the capital where he remained until his final and ill-fated tour of 211 B.C.

It is easy to pass judgment on the inspections of Shihuang and to conjecture on his final frenzied search for immortality. But his motives, clouded as they later became, were clear in the beginning. He wanted to inspect his realm and to inform the Blackhaired people that a new era of peace had been inaugurated. And he wanted to show, beyond any doubt, that he was in control.

The state of Qin succeeded in obtaining eight of the nine sacred tripods of the House of Zhou in 255 B.C.; the last one eluded the grasp of the First Emperor.

Shihuang was so successful in all his endeavors that later artists could only attribute his failure to obtain the sacred tripods to the intervention of supernatural opponents. Here, a dragon severs the cord being used to raise the tripod.

The Gods of Shihuang

AT THE BEGINNING OF his reign, Shihuang worshipped the "Four Gods" – the *di* associated with colours, animals, and the elements. Red represented fire, and blue-green, the dragon; white, the tiger; and yellow, the earth or the sun.

The slaughtered animals offered to these gods were either burnt so that the rising smoke united the heavens to the earth, or buried, in the belief that they would reach the gods below. During this period we hear of many sorts of blood sacrifices – calves, sheep, white dogs, horses, etc., but there was a gradual tendency in Shihuang's time to replace them with effigies – the "straw dogs" mentioned by the philosopher, Lao Zi.

Shihuang's tours were also conducted for religious reasons. The Chinese word for this sort of tour – *xunshou* means not only to follow a road, but also to "shepherd" or "care for." An emperor on tour represented Heaven, demonstrated his love for his subjects, and by visiting and making sacrifices at various sites, also performed his own pilgrimage. Burnt offerings were made at many of these sites where the emperor consulted with local notables and officials, often correcting their calendars so they would accord with the Heavenly Seasons which it was his prerogative to define.

Shihuang's long inscriptions were also primarily of religious significance. Yes, they may have served a political purpose with their emphasis on his achievements of peace and unification, and yes, they may have been his legacy to the ages, demanding that future generations marvel at what he had done. "Great and manifest," he said in his first inscription, "is the virtue of the Sovereign Emperor. It is to be handed down to generations yet to come. Without change." But above all, his inscriptions were an announcement to Heaven of his deeds and a prayer that Heaven would continue to bless him. That is why he would proclaim, in the same inscription, (219 B.C.) that he rose early and went late to bed, tirelessly labouring for the sake of his people. He was assuring Heaven that his people "celebrated his virtue," and that Heaven should therefore permit his rule to continue.

Shihuang's tours took him almost always to the northeast, to present-day Shandong province, which in those days was probably more sophisticated, more learned and more mystical in its religious beliefs than any other part of China. It was the home of Confucius and of Zou Yan, the philosopher to whom is attributed the formulation of the Five Element theory; and it was the site of Mount Tai, the most sacred of mountains.

Here he met with the learned men of the area. Here, too, he performed several rites, many of them devoted to the so-called "Eight Spirits," or *ba-shen*, whom the *Shiji* tells us, had long been neglected. The interesting thing about these observances is that he did not sacrifice equally to the Eight, but chose three for special worship: the God of the *Yang* Force, the Lord of the

The Taoist pantheon was a huge one, still in the process of formation in the time of Shihuang.

Pictured here are representative Taoist deities which once adorned the walls of a Yuan dynasty temple.

Four Seasons, and the Lord of the Sun.

The active *Yang* force, from the dim beginnings of this cosmology, had been the complement of the receptive *Yin* force, both forces interacting, eternally changing and melding to create a cosmic harmony. Probably by Qin times, dozens of other associations had clustered around these forces – male and female, father and son, heaven and earth, sun and moon, etc. But *Yang* was always the vital force, the creator, the initiator.

At the beginning of the new year, Shihuang worshipped The God of the Four Seasons at Langyai, his favourite site. The Lord of the Sun was also worshipped nearby, at a temple located on a promontory beneath Mount Zheng, where Shihuang could watch the sun rise from the sea.

Shihuang worshipped the gods of the beginning, the moment of creation, the gods who best represented his own self-image.

The Purposes of Shihuang's Rituals

IF SHIHUANG'S INTEREST IN beginnings reflects his awareness of his historical role, it also reflects something else. The beginning of each day is the morning, the fresh and uncluttered time, the time of rejuvenation and the awakening of life. By the time Shihuang unified "All under Heaven" in 221 B.C., he was only thirty-eight years old. But since the age of thirteen, he had been under siege: thrust as a boy onto the throne of a major state contending for supreme power; manipulated by his "Second Father," Lu Buwei; betrayed by his mother; the target of an assassination which almost succeeded; and year-by-year, the director of campaigns which meant life or death to his state. He was tired. But as China's First Unifier, his work had just begun. It is little wonder that on his tours, he also sought rejuvenation for himself. And that he sought immortality.

The search for immortality is a recurrent and constant theme in Shihuang's life, and it helps to explain many of the more puzzling of his religious observances. Scholars have often wondered, for instance, why he forbade, by decree, the worship of the "Bright Star" (Venus). The simple explanation is probably the fact that from his capital, it was most often seen in the west, the direction associated with the autumn season and with impending death. He did not want to be reminded of his own mortality nor to think of the end of his life.

As the *Shiji* tells us, Shihuang sacrificed to no fewer than eighteen mountains and seventeen rivers, and at hundreds of shrines in the vicinity of the capital. There were shrines to the gods of the sun and the moon, to the various planets, to the winds and the rains, and to a variety of other natural forces which would ensure that the Heavenly Seasons were regular. Shihuang had decreed from the time of his unification, that the variant sacrifices would all be unified, that "the various officials in charge of sacrifices put into order the worship of Heaven and Earth, the famous mountains and the great rivers, as well as the other spirits who had customarily been honoured in the past." Thus, he demanded that the rivers thawed on time and that the grain ripened when it should. Sacrifices of cows and calves, and of jade and silk ensured that this would happen, and more than that, ensured that Shihuang would himself live to see his full seasons.

And always, there was the search for the herbs and drugs which would bring him immortality.

It is difficult to know with precision just what Shihuang's ideas were on the afterlife, since nowhere, except perhaps in his still-to-be opened tomb, is there explicit evidence. We do, however, know a good deal about the ideas of life and death which were current in his time since we have much evidence about them in the literature of the Han dynasty, a period not too long after his death.

The basic belief was that human beings had two souls, called the *hun* and the *po*. Combining in man's material body, they harmonized to create the spark of life, and were separated only at death. The *hun* directed the intellect and the spiritual activity, while the *po* directed movement and physical activity. At death, the *hun* proceeded either to a vague realm of ancestors and spirits called *di*, or sometimes *xian* or immortals. This realm was somewhere aloft, invisible to human eyes, but still below Heaven. The immortals drank from rivers of jade and ate the fruit of magical trees, and sometimes, they came back to the earth to pluck the Herbs of Immortality found on the highest mountain-tops. The *po*, on the other hand, stayed with the corpse for a long time and unless the proper rituals of the dead were performed, could wander the earth as a *quei* or a hungry ghost. The prophecy that Shihuang's empire would be destroyed by *Hu* was delivered by one of these ghosts.

The yang *force is pictured in many ways. One of the most common is the vibrant red crown of the crane of longevity. Shihuang often worshipped this* yang *force.*

The Land of Immortals

SHIHUANG AND HIS PEOPLE believed that there were men living on earth who had prolonged their lives forever by the ingestion of magic herbs, or by potions and elixirs. During the Qin period these immortals were to be found in the Blessed Isles of the Eastern Sea, and in later times, in the mountainous realm of the Queen Mother of the West. Our fullest early description of the Blessed Isles dates from about the third century A.D. but clearly draws upon much earlier mythology, and certainly upon Shihuang's own beliefs.

East of Bohai, we know not how many thousands and millions of leagues away, there is a mighty abyss, in truth the bottomless vale, with no base beneath and named "The Way to the Void." The water from the eight corners and the nine divisions of the universe... all flow into this valley which grows neither larger nor smaller. There are five mountains there...[which] measure thirty thousand leagues in height and in girth, and there is a flat plain at the summit which stretches for nine-thousand leagues.... The terraces and towers at the top are all made of gold and jade; the animals and birds are all pure white. Trees of pearls and precious gems flourish there, with flowers and fruits of a delicious taste. None of those who eat of them grow old or die, and the beings who live there are... immortal beings and holy men. In the course of a single day and night, they fly from one island to another, times without number.

The passage goes on to say that the mountains were free-floating until anchored on the backs of giant turtles, perhaps

the very beasts which prevented Shihuang's magicians from landing on the isles in 211 B.C.! Another tradition had it that when human beings approached, the mountains would recede and disappear like a mirage, but Shihuang's magicians did not dare to use this excuse with him. Their very lives depended upon their ability to convince him that the herbs could be obtained.

What, then, are we to make of Shihuang's never-ending search for immortality? He was a practical man, not a gullible one. He demanded results from his other officials and swiftly punished those who failed or who showed incompetence. But he showed a strange leniency toward his alchemists and magicians. Books of divination were excluded from the burning of the books in 213 B.C., and the investigation of those scholars

Sacred mountains and mountain-top worship in China is a very ancient tradition. In fact, the legendary sage-king, Yao, is said to have been the first to make a ritual circuit of the "Five Sacred Mountains" as early as 2346 B.C. As in other cultures, mountain-tops were seen as the meeting-place of Heaven and earth and the dwelling-place of benevolent spirits.

In China, the five peaks which Shihuang ascended marked the boundaries of the Chinese world in mythological times and he made sacrifices on them to show that he had restored unity. He wished also to demonstrate that he was the highest of all human beings, extending his domain to the north, south, east and west.

buried the next year was restricted to those who resided in the capital. Purposely, it seems, he spared those like Xu Shi, who were stationed on the eastern coast to oversee the search for the Blessed Isles.

Three explanations of his search for immortality are possible. The first is that Shihuang needed time. Although he had accomplished so much, he was acutely aware that there was more to do, that the changes he had wrought were still fragile and impermanent. His activities heightened rather than slackened in the last years of his life, and increasingly, he placed less trust in those around him. He refused until the very last moment even to designate an heir! Thus, in order to complete his tasks, he needed to live on.

A second explanation, and one which may be just as likely, is that he accepted the reality of a physical death but wished to live on as a god. He wanted the institution of emperor, which after all, he had created, to be godlike. His very title, *huangdi*, set him above ordinary mortals, and in his inscriptions, we find references to his "divine power," his "brilliant holiness," and his ability to influence even the fertility of the beasts of the field. Within a century of his death, the institution of the Chinese Emperor did indeed, take on godlike characteristics, and this was assuredly among the most important of his political legacies.

And there is the final possibility: Shihuang, at the end of his life, simply lost his perspective, and his grasp on reality. He succumbed, like so many figures of towering achievement, to a megalomania which made him look for a way to live forever.

The Royal Roads

THE IMPERIAL INSPECTIONS OF Shihuang could not have been accomplished without the great road network he had built, remnants of which still exist today. Some modern highways in China parallel or follow the roadways Shihuang began in 220 B.C.

Again, these projects were an integral part of the unification of Shihuang's empire. The roads radiated from the capital like wheel-spokes and were called "fast-roads." They were built by convicts and conscripts under close direction from the emperor who demanded progress at any cost, human or material.

Made of packed earth and very wide, they were decorated with willow trees placed at intervals alongside them. Near the capital, there are indications even of a centre lane reserved strictly for imperial use.

Today, the roads of Shihuang would be called expressways or throughways. In his time, they were even more remarkable because he had standardized the axles of carts and chariots to ensure that the ruts in the roads were uniform, the better to make them stand up to wear and tear.

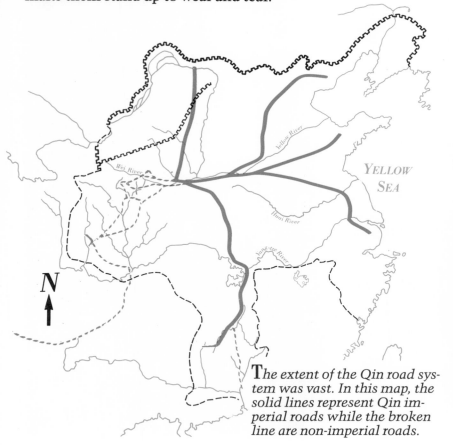

The extent of the Qin road system was vast. In this map, the solid lines represent Qin imperial roads while the broken line are non-imperial roads.

In 212 B.C., Shihuang ordered his finest general, Meng Tian, the builder of the Great Wall, to construct a north-south artery from his summer palace north of Xianyang far into present-day Mongolia. This so-called "straight road" can still be seen today near a modern highway.

In total, the royal roads of Shihuang covered about 4,250 miles, thus exceeding by 500 miles the Roman road system as it existed 350 years later.

They stimulated commercial development, tied the empire together and helped bring about the tax surpluses suggested by the *Shiji* which records that in 214 B.C., Shihuang felt wealthy enough to bestow to each village, as a year-end gift, a certain quantity of rice and two sheep.

There were other huge construction projects during the time of Shihuang which also contributed to the prosperity of the period.

First were canals and irrigation works designed to stimulate agriculture and transport grain and goods.

Shihuang was responsible for three large canal projects, two of them begun around the time he came to the throne in 246 B.C. The first was the Zhengguo canal. The man who first suggested it was an engineer from the rival state of Han who hoped that the project would not only take the Qin rulers' minds off war but also exhaust the state's resources.

Ironically, the effect was quite the opposite. The *Shiji* remarks:

"And thus the lands of Qin within the passes were turned into a fertile plain and there were no more years of famine. Qin became strong and rich, and in the end, overcame the various feudal lords."

The second canal was the Dujiang Weir and it was built in the southwest on the Chengdu plain in Sichuan province. This was a hinterland in Qin times and the Weir became so important that the canal has been constantly kept in repair and today waters China's most populous province.

The final canal was begun around 219 B.C. and was originally designed to transport supplies to the armies in the south. This three-mile canal was built through mountains to connect the Xiang and the Li Rivers, both tributaries of the Yangtze. It formed a crucial link between them and is still in use today.

But the roads paled before Shihuang's other major engineering feat – the Great Wall of China, a monument or, if you will, a barrier to barbarism that will always be associated with the name of the First Emperor.

Although this detail of a long Chinese scroll painting shows the celebration of the spring festival along a river, we can imagine that such gaiety became part of Chinese life along the canals.

Shihuang's irrigation systems contributed to the fertility of the land.

The Building of the Great Wall

ANY DESCRIPTION OF THE Great Wall of China must begin with China's past. Seven principalities in the Warring States period had constructed walls to protect their northern borders and when Shihuang ordered the Great Wall, it was both a consolidation of earlier walls and an extension.

The Wall should also be associated with the name of General Meng Tian who was given this huge task in 221 B.C. when he was ordered to protect the northern frontier of the empire from the nomadic steppe tribes. To carry out his work, he was given an army of more than 300,000 men who simultaneously fought the "barbarians," constructed roads and built

General Meng Tian, the architect of the Great Wall.

the Great Wall. Thousands of convicts were also sent to the Great Wall for forced labor punishment.

It took Meng Tian ten years to finish the wall and it was a mammoth achievement, stretching uninterrupted for more than ten thousand *li*, or about 4,100 kilometres (2,600 miles). This is considerably longer than the Wall today which is estimated to have an overall length of 3,400 kilometres or 2,150 miles.

Whether sections fell or the early Chinese over-estimated the length we do not know. But the engineering involved, the incredible logistics of conquering large sections of mountains, of transporting materials and even crossing semi-deserts, is almost incomprehensible.

For every man working on the wall, ten must have been assigned to build the roads and transport the supplies to it. The men worked through brutally cold winters, and through blazing summers. There was little rest and the death toll must have been enormous.

Unlike such stationary constructions as the sphinxes, pyramids and other monumental wonders of the ancient world, wall-building required every skill in the engineer's repertoire.

As the contours of the land changed, so too did the logistics of erecting the Wall. And as the Wall progressed, the lines of supply became longer and transportation became more and more difficult.

Natural obstacles had to be removed or circled without the help of the kind of equipment or explosives that would be used today. The terrain transversed by the Wall includes the marshes and quicksand of the Ordos region and the semi-desert conditions of the east. In one area, the wall was built at a height of 6,000 feet above sea level.

In addition to the extreme climate and inclement weather conditions, the laborers were subject to attack and harassment from the marauding nomads as well as to the constant urgings from Meng Tian to build faster, faster, faster.

Included in the many thousands who died were soldiers and conscript laborers, convicts, prisoners of war, magistrates who failed in their duties and even scholars who had refused to surrender their books for burning. Many were buried within the wall itself, and we shall never know the exact number. One clue is the frequent reference by Chinese historians to the "Wall of Tears" or to the "Longest Graveyard in the World."

Qin unified and extended existing walls to create the Great Wall of China.

Tales of the Great Wall

THERE ARE MYRIAD TALES about the building of the Great Wall. One says Shihuang was told by a magician that the Wall could not be completed until "ten-thousand" (*wan*) had been buried in it.

Shihuang then found a man whose given name contained the word "ten-thousand" and had him killed and interred in the wall so the work could proceed.

In another tale, it is said Shihuang himself became a magician and travelled to the moon, the better to survey the land and plan the course of the Wall. While there, he received a miraculous whip to cut down the mountains, stay the flow of the rivers and drive the miserable workers to even greater efforts.

Still another legend gives Shihuang a magic black horse with a red mane and eyes which glowed in the dark. The horse dredged out the earth with his saddle dragging behind him, and the workmen followed his meandering course as they built the Wall. This accounts for its curves and twists.

There are ghost stories about the Wall also and we find, in dynasty after dynasty, poets who lament the suffering caused by its construction. And there are simple poignant stories told even today to those who visit the Wall.

One of the best-known stories concerns a beautiful princess. When her state fell to Shihuang in the last days of unification, her husband was condemned to work on the Wall where he died and was buried, like many others, inside it.

Seeking his body, the princess, after a long and dangerous journey, finally reached the Wall but found that no one could find her husband's body among so many corpses.

Devastated, she was preparing to return home when a spirit appeared to her. The spirit told her to cut her hand and walk along the length of the Wall. The blood would form a trail and lead her to the resting place of her beloved husband. She obeyed the spirit's instructions and found her husband's body, taking it from the Wall and back to her home for proper burial.

Legends aside, the Wall has fascinated people for generations.

For a while during the seventeenth century, there was fierce debate about when the Wall was built. Why, for example, did Marco Polo who visited China in the thirteenth century, not mention it?

Some other scholars said the Wall was not erected until after the Mongols had left China. Archaeology came to the rescue, and Shihuang's achievements were duly recognized. As for Marco Polo, it was later realized that he entered China by a route which would not have taken him through the Wall.

Many popular beliefs – like the legends – are pure myth. The wall cannot be seen from outer space, nor from the moon. It is also not continuous and it is not built entirely from stone. Nevertheless, it is an astounding monument to one man and his dynasty.

The First Emperor maps his wall in sand.

Not a solid rampart of earth or stone like the Roman walls in northern England, the Great Wall was laid on stone foundations or solid rock, and made of hard-baked brick with a clay filling between. Brick platforms were built on top, crowned by parapets.

The *Shiji* does not tell us if the Wall was built in a continuous line or by two distinct parties of workers who started at each end and eventually met in the middle. The upper surface of the Wall was built to allow rainwater to drain off, and there were loopholes for archers in the parapets.

Every few hundred yards, a watchtower rose above the wall to provide cross-fire in the case of attack. When the wall was complete, there were 2,500 such towers, each 40 feet square and 40 feet high.

The sinuous outline of the wall resembles a writhing dragon.

"The Ten Thousand Mile Long Wall," the common Chinese name for the Great Wall.

Watchtowers were built at intervals along the Great Wall.

DYNASTY

The Emperor's Palaces

OTHER CONSTRUCTIONS DESIGNED to enhance the majesty of the Emperor Shihuang are still clouded in mystery because little detail is available from traditional Chinese sources. Each year, however, new archaeological finds show more and more the grandeur of his work even though the interior of his tomb had not yet been opened.

The first reference to Shihuang's constructions occur in the *Shiji* under the year 221 and are not mentioned again until the year 212 B.C. In the year of the dynastic proclamation, 221 B.C., it is said that he began the enhancement of the capital with the mansions for his defeated enemies.

According to the *Shiji*, he ordered huge galleries, connecting walkways, and magnificent parks and gardens. But it is not clear if this was an ongoing process or accomplished quickly with a huge force of laborers.

Then, the second passage of the *Shiji* states that in 212 B.C., Shihuang started a new building project.

"And then, Shihuang made up his mind that the population of Xianyang had grown large while the royal palaces of his ancestors were still small. He said: 'I have heard that the (sage kings) Wen and Wu of Zhou had their capitals at Fong and Hao.

" 'The region between them is suitable for a capital for emperors and kings.' "

Shihuang then began building new throne palaces south of the Wei River in the middle of the Shanglin Park. He first build the Front Palace, the Afang (whose name means "beside the capital") and its huge dimensions were obviously designed to impress the magnificence of Shihuang's new dynasty on all who saw it.

The Afang measured 675 metres east to west and 112 metres north to south. The galleries, it is said, could hold 10,000 persons, and from the floor to the ceiling, banners fifty feet high could stand.

A huge causeway wide enough for horses circled the palace

阿 房 宮

The name of Qin Shihuang's palace – Afang – written in Chinese.

The opulence and grandeur of the palaces of Qin Shihuang.

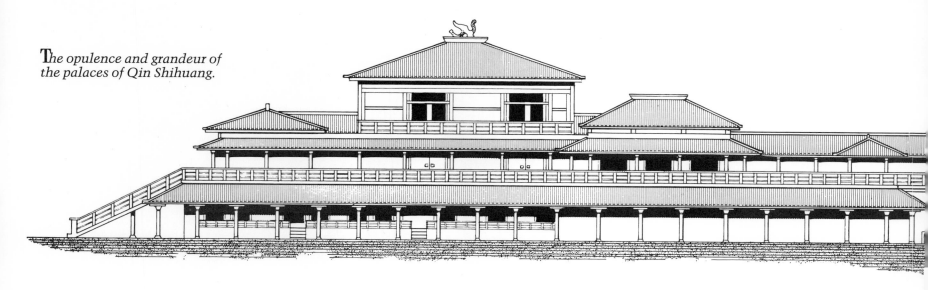

and climbed to the South Mountain to end in a triumphal arch on the top. Another road bridged the Wei River and entered Xianyang to symbolize the corridor of stars which crosses the Milky Way from the constellation known as the Apex of Heaven to the Constellation of the Royal Chamber.

More than 700,000 men, many of them castrated prisoners, were sent to work on the Afang site and the neighboring mausoleum at Mount Li.

Quarried stone and special woods and timber beams were transported from the south and southwest. And, the *Shiji* says, there were three hundred palaces built within the original Qin homeland in the Wei River Valley and more than four hundred outside.

Some of Shihuang's building efforts were driven more by fear than by a desire to impress. In the year 212 B.C., two years before his death, Shihuang was approached by a frightened magician who offered the following explanation for his failure to find the elixir of the immortals. He told Shihuang that evil spirits were everywhere and the emperor must escape them by keeping his whereabouts secret. The emperor must become almost invisible, he warned him, or the secret of immortality would never be his.

Further, the magician said, his future divinity would be threatened if his ministers or subjects knew where he was. Shihuang, obviously desperate now for immortality, believed all this and ordered a network of secret passages and covered roadways built to connect the 270 palaces and pavilions.

Attention was given to the smaller details as can be seen in the intricacy of these roof tile ends.

The *Shiji* concludes the passage by saying:

"After this time, no one knew where he was. When he dealt with official matters, he presented his ministers only with what he had already decided, and all was determined within his Xianyang palaces."

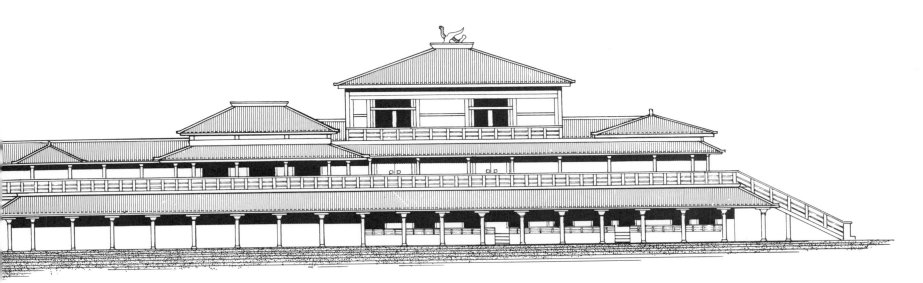

Prelude to the Fall of Qin

OW WAS IT THAT Qin Shihuang could carry out such massive construction throughout his land in such a short period of time?

Although scholars of pre-modern China are accustomed to the numerical exaggerations in the ancient records, the figures given for the conscript and convict labour used on the Great Wall and for Shihuang's other building projects, may not be too far off the mark. For only by massive and cruel impressment of labour could he have achieved such rapid results.

As he watched a new world arise around him, a world he himself had planned and realized, how godlike he must have felt! Meanwhile, his subjects, the Blackhaired people, were living with the consequences of Shihuang's godlike ambition.

Although from 221 B.C. until his death, China had enjoyed widespread domestic peace, this had not meant that the farmer was left in peace to till his fields. Troops must have been levied for General Meng Tian's garrisons encamped along the outer borders where he "awed and terrified the Xiongnu," and also for the campaigns which from 214 B.C. onward added new territory to the Empire in the south so that China began to approach its modern territorial extent. To accomplish these conquests the troops must have been conscripted from the farmers of the land.

Nor did Shihuang have any compunction about moving ordinary civilians to territories which he felt were in need of colonization. He sent more than 30,000 households – most unwillingly – to the Langyai area after his first visit there in 219 B.C. and, as his military campaigns became more intensive, he sent other families to populate new territorial acquisitions.

The *Shiji* says he sent enough people to the north to establish thirty-five counties and he ordered merchants and bond-servants to the south. In 213 B.C., more families were sent to populate areas near the Great Wall and to support the construction work there.

In 212 B.C., when his attention turned to building projects closer to home, he ordered another 30,000 families to Mount Li to work on his tomb, and another 50,000 were sent to his summer palace, the southern terminus of the great road moving north from that point.

The year before his death, Shihuang moved another 30,000 families to the Ordos region and although each received an advance of one degree of honorary rank, there was still a growing chorus of protest rising against the vast upheaval of the common people. As a family consisted usually of five per-sons during this period, large numbers of people were affected each time the emperor spoke – not only those who were transported but their relatives who were left behind.

After centuries of warfare, the peace Shihuang's Blackhaired people had dreamt of, the chance to raise their families, was still not in sight. Under the First Emperor's regime, more and more people felt their dream would never come true, and discontent swept across the land.

A *mood of melancholy fell across the land in the last years of Shihuang's reign.*

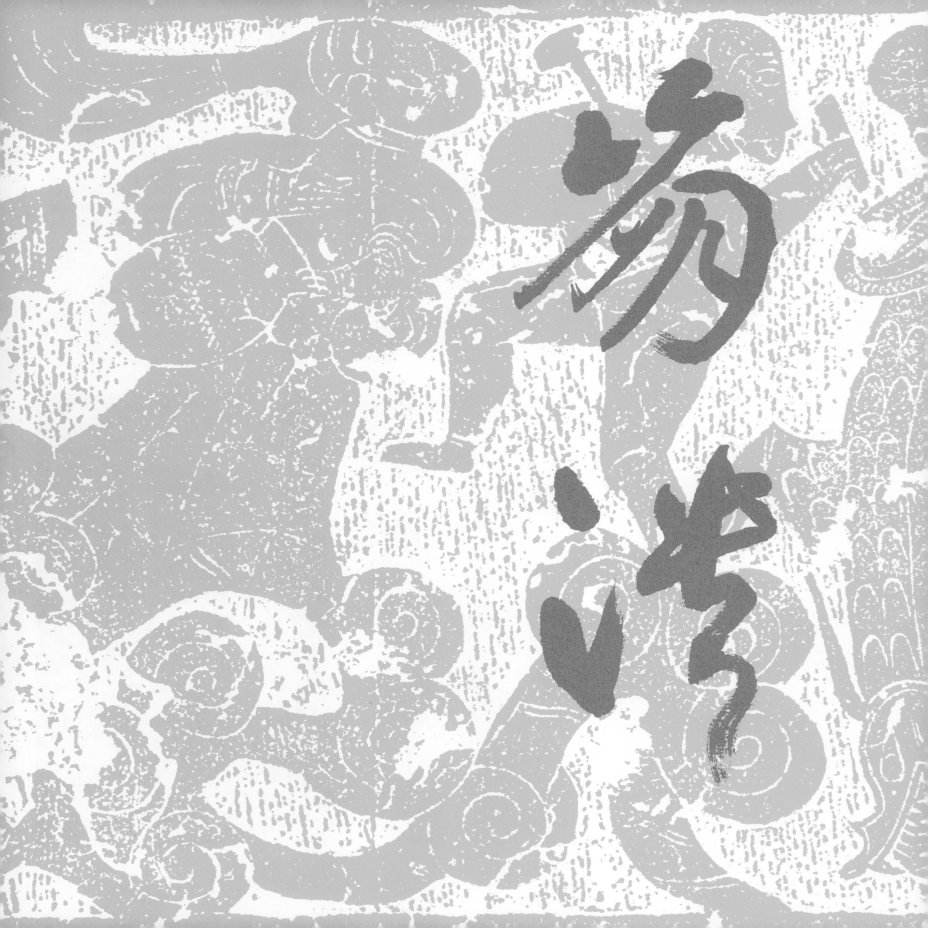

The Death Of The Primal Dragon

The Fall of the Qin Dynasty

The Great Debate

CHINESE POLITICAL THEORY during Shihuang's reign took the position that a ruler held the empire by a mandate from Heaven, and when he ceased to follow the mandate, Heaven sent omens and portents to warn him to change his ways.

By 215 B.C., Shihuang was displaying more and more the signs of meglomania and paranoia that were to mark his later years. The educated courtiers began to whisper of Heaven's disapproval in that year, and the *Shiji* records the first sign of a crack in his iron rule.

A magician, Magister Lu, returned from a fruitless search for the elixir of immortality and presented to Shihuang a book he had supposedly obtained from a Taoist immortal. Lu claimed the book contained the first prediction of the fall of Qin.

The text said the cause of Qin's overthrow would be *"Hu,"* a term usually used to refer to the Xiongnu barbarians in the north. Shihuang reacted quickly and sent new forces against them to stay the prophecy.

But Shihuang forgot that his favorite son who later became his heir also had the word *"Hu"* in his name. Later events, despite the acceleration of warfare and the hardship it caused, would prove the prophecy true.

Shihuang's reaction to the warning was typical of his rule. Instead of interpreting it as a sign from Heaven to change his ways, he retaliated with his war machine and attempted to destroy the threat. This stopped the palace couriers' mumbling for a while, but within two years, a much more serious protest arose and Shihuang would shock the empire with his dangerous and impetuous actions.

Early in the year 213 B.C., the emperor gave a banquet in the palace to celebrate his birth and invited his seventy "scholars of wide learning." Among these officials were numerous sycophants all too ready to flatter the emperor, wish him a long life and write flowery tributes to his greatness.

Most followed this script but there was a dissenting opinion, almost unheard of in previous days and yet another sign of a widening crack in Shihuang's control.

A scholar called Yue boldly suggested at the banquet that the reason the earlier dynasties had survived for so long was because of the distribution of lands to favoured members of the ruling house and meritorious ministers who, in turn, set up loyal tributaries.

Survival of the Qin, Yue contended, depended upon an ability to learn from the past.

Although carefully couched in scholarly terms, this was a direct rebuke to Shihuang's centralized, non-feudal form of government and it seemed to have stunned the emperor. But he carefully listened to the thesis and called for a debate on the subject.

He, of course, would make the final decision.

And it was Li Si, the paramount minister, who presented the counter-argument to Yue, at the same time proposing a bold policy which would have ramifications in China for the next 2,200 years.

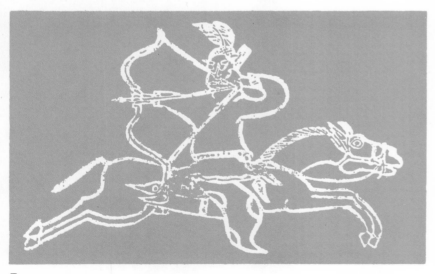

In *Shihuang's time, China's nomadic neighbours were called the* hu.

Throughout Chinese history the quest for immortality was pervasive. This Qing dynasty plate shows a mountaintop dwelling of the immortals.

The Burning of the Books

AS THE EMPEROR SAT LISTENING on the throne with his ministers and scholars gathered below him in the banquet hall, Li Si claimed that the kings and Sons of Heaven of the previous dynasties did not copy each other but instead, innovated new laws in response to the needs of the time. Only the foolish failed to understand this.

The Qin dynasty was a new era, Li Si went on, a time when *"all the laws and all decrees issue from a single source, when the 'Blackhaired people' support themselves by farming and handicrafts and students study only the laws and prohibitions."*

In short, Qin had become a utopia, the perfect embodiment of Legalist state-theory. Then Li Si became more vitriolic, turning his criticism against the scholars themselves, men he intimated were fomenting revolution in the minds of the people.

"They study the past in order to criticize the times in which we live," he said, *"and they sow confusion among the Black-haired people. Speaking frankly, and on pain of death, I cannot but say that in the past, when the world was torn by chaos and disorder, no one could unify it.*

"That is why so many would-be rulers arose, using the past

to *denigrate the present, burying reality in their empty arguments and rhetoric."*

Li Si warned the emperor that *"there are those who condemn your laws and your orders, and as soon as they hear that a decree has been issued, they debate its merits according to their own school of thought, opposing it secretly in their hearts at court and disputing it openly in the streets.*

"This lowers the prestige of the sovereign and leads to the formation of factions below. It must be stopped."

Then Li Si stunned the court by offering a proposition that

Medical treatises were spared from Shihuang's book burning, and archeological evidence shows that by this time, these works were both numerous and detailed. One example, a silk roll recently unearthed in Hunan province, dates from a period prior to the unification, and lists no fewer than 100 medical conditions, with over 300 treatments described which use 240 different herbal preparations. The silk roll also depicts more than 40 exercises for the prevention of various diseases, pre-dating our emphasis on jogging and aerobics by almost 2500 years.

Qin Shihuang attempted to destroy the literary heritage of his people.

would one day be seen as the beginning of the end of the Qin dynasty, a proposition so startling that historians for centuries have vilified Shihuang for agreeing to it.

"All the official histories of the contending states, except the annals of Qin should be burned. Anyone who possesses the (Confucian) Book of Odes *and the* Book of History *or the philosophical discourses of the hundred schools must present them to the proper civil authorities for burning."*

Anyone who "dared" to discuss the works in public would be executed, Li Si suggested, and their bodies left exposed for all to see. Anyone who refused the edict would have his face tattooed and be sent to forced labor on the Great Wall, a penalty which in many cases amounted to a sentence of death.

The only exceptions to the burning – in essence the destruction of many centuries of Chinese thought – were books on medicine and pharmacy, divination, agriculture and forestry.

Shihuang agreed with this favoured minister and put the decree into effect. The books were burned, a fiery cleansing which was designed to preserve the empire but instead, eventually helped to destroy it.

To speak of "books" in the time of Shihuang is something of a misnomer since the Chinese did not invent true paper until 105 A.D. Prior to that, silk was used, but because it was still scarce and expensive, wooden strips were far more common. The "books" which Shihuang burned were probably in this form.

To make a "book", the wood was first dried of sap, then cut and planed into thin strips of standard length, usually about 50 cm. long. Characters were usually written on one side only, and then the strips were bound with hemp which was passed through grooves designed to preserve the proper order of the "pages." The whole thing was rolled up like a rug for storage and transport. Official documents and imperial edicts were also dispatched in this form, but only after the strings were covered with clay and the proper seal affixed. When the clay hardened, the document could not be tampered with until it reached its proper destination.

The Execution of the Scholars

SO FEARFUL HAD THE ATMOSPHERE in the palace become that even Shihuang's three hundred official astronomers – employed to observe the movements of the Heavens – did not dare to report any unfavorable omens.

Nervous and irritable, Shihuang surrounded himself with flatterers who did little but offer flowery speeches of respect. He felt increasingly that he could trust no one, and he took upon his own shoulders the entire weight of administration. The *Shiji* tells us that he had documents of state weighed morning and night, not sleeping until 120 pounds had passed through his hands.

He also continued blindly to send out officials to discover the Island of the Immortals and the elixir of life. None succeeded, but Shihuang was convinced that if he found the magical herbs, he could live forever.

He was, perhaps, slowly going mad. Certainly, by 212 B.C., he was highly frustrated by the failure of his soothsayers to synthesize the elixir or to reach the Islands of the Immortals. And he was impatient about the costs. When two of the magicians absconded, he was in a rage, and said,

"Now I learn that these many magicians have departed without warning, having spent millions with no results. I have showered them with honors and yet they slander me, reproaching me with my faults.

"I have had enquiries made about the scholars who consorted with these magicians and find that they are spreading vicious rumors in the capital to confuse the Blackhaired people."

With that, Shihuang ordered a full judicial inquiry into the hunt for immortality and the role of the scholars. He appeared to be convinced his magicians were in collusion with scholars who did not wish to see him succeed in his quest for eternal life.

He called together the scholars and when they were assembled – *"all scrambling one to incriminate the other,"* as the *Shiji* records it – he personally selected 460 of them to use as an example. All were put to a horrible death.

The method of execution was called *keng*, a term which can mean "live burial," and though recent scholarship disputes this interpretation, the Chinese have always believed that the scholars were literally buried alive from the neck down.

The Chinese people have always believed that the scholars were buried alive.

This horrifying act, coming within a year of the book burning, further shocked the people and became etched forever in Chinse history, determining that Shihuang would be seen as a cruel and unreasoning despot. These two acts overshadowed his achievements.

The execution of the scholars also divided the emperor's own family. His eldest son, Fu Su, dared to oppose the decree, warning his father that the act would be ultimately destructive to the dynasty, and was not worth the short-term gains. The emperor again went into a dark rage and banished Fu Su to the Great Wall, sending with him the last group of terrified scholars.

No one, not even the heir-apparent among his many children, could criticize the Tiger Emperor with impunity.

▷**I**n this Qing dynasty painting, Qin Shihuang oversees the burning of the books and the burying of the scholars. Sometime after this painting was made the eyes of the First Emperor were scratched out.

焚書坑儒

"*He burned the books and buried the scholars*" *has become a common expression in China.*

Fear of "The Dragon"

SHIHUANG'S BOOK-BURNING was not the first in Chinese history, nor would it be the last. The great literary inquisition of the Quianlong Emperor from 1772-88 A.D. was far more destructive, and the frequent sacking of imperial libraries in times of rebellion or dynastic change also cost the Chinese people many great works.

But, nevertheless, no event in Qin history so gripped the minds of later generations.

It was the first universal act of philistinism among a people who venerated literature and philosophy and it came at a time when books were rare and precious things — hand-copied with painstaking care.

The fragile legacy of the past, the annals of a people in the process of melding and forming their own identity, was summarily lost. And of course, many of the books consigned to the flames were attributed to Confucius and others who were to become the sages of later eras for the Chinese people. Most of the works were not canonical in Qin times, but later came to be regarded with such reverence, that their destruction was regarded with even greater horror.

The burning had extreme ramifications, both practical and symbolic. The edict was not formally revoked until 191 B.C. and much of the intellectual life of the next dynasty was devoted to reconstruction through the oral tradition of the prohibited texts and also through copies said to have been successfully hidden, though some were obviously forgeries.

It took almost four centuries, until 175 A.D., to reach consensus on recognized versions and even today, scholars debate the authenticity of most of these "classics." All agree, however, that Shihuang's actions signalled the end of the Golden Age of Chinese thought.

There was soon to follow another dark event that was to become associated with the burning of the books, an event almost as terrible, and one which became part of every Chinese vocabulary: *"Shihuang burned the books and buried the scholars."*

It occurred in 212 B.C., a year later and long after the thirty days specified by Shihuang for scholars to turn in their books. It came at a time when the emperor was beginning his new northern highway and conscripting 700,000 men to work on the Afang palace and on his mausoleum.

It also came at a time when Magister Lu, now gaining greater control over the emperor with his magic and omens, convinced Shihuang to hide himself from mortal eyes and move secretly among the 270 sleeping palaces he had newly-constructed precisely for that purpose.

As his thoughts became ever more closely focussed on his own mortality, Shihuang was becoming more imperious and cruel. On one occasion, it is said, he looked down from his palace wall and, seeing the huge retinue which surrounded Li Si, complained to his ministers that Li Si was becoming too proud. He had begun to mistrust his only true ally.

When Li Si heard of the comment, he dutifully acknowledged it and diminished the size of his entourage. This enraged Shihuang, who knew that someone around him had told Li Si of his remarks. So he had everyone who had been with him on that day seized and put to death, without the usual trial.

Within the palace walls the courtiers became extremely nervous and the magicians and sorcerers secretly began to accuse Shihuang of cruelty, intimidation and megalomania. The atmosphere of the court became poisonous with fear.

The Chinese have many ways of representing the character shou, meaning "long life." It adorns everything from textiles to porcelain, from greeting cards to tea cups.

"Penglai", one of the Isles of the immortals.

As Shihuang grew older, his interest in preserving his life grew more intense. The Isle of the Immortals beckoned ever more strongly.

A Portent of Death

THE EROSION OF MORALE continued, however, and now even the heavens conspired with the doomsayers who said the time of Shihuang was rapidly coming to an end. Mars entered the constellation known as the Scorpion's Heart, a most unfavourable placement in the minds of those who watched the skies. And a meteor fell flaming to earth. By the time it was examined by the court astrologers, someone had inscribed upon it the words:

"After the death of the Primal Dragon, the empire will be divided."

When this terrible divination was brought before him, Shihuang panicked and sent out spies to find the author of the cryptic – and telling – message. When the hunt failed, Shihaung quickly had everyone in the area where the meteor had fallen put to death by beheading.

This act of cruelty is followed in the *Shiji* with the words, *"He was unable to find happiness."* Shihuang became more tormented and deathly afraid. He trusted no one; none of his obsequious followers could win his favour. He spent long and lonely hours wandering through his vast palaces, reading documents and pacing through the vast halls.

But he continued to try to manipulate his fate and delay his impending death. His few remaining scholars, most of them terrified now to make a wrong move, still tried to interpret the emperor's incoherent thoughts. After the incident of the meteor, they were ordered to compose poems of praise to the immortals. When they were accepted after due ceremony, Shihuang had them set to music and ordered them to be sung and played to him every night while he pored through the endless documents from his magistrates and governors. He began to refer to himself as the "Perfected Being," one who was immortal, insisting that his courtiers refer to him in that way.

Then came another omen. The *Shiji* writes that an imperial envoy was accosted one night by a mysterious figure who

handed him a jade tally for the emperor and said: *"In this year, the First Emperor will die."* The figure, according to legend, then dissolved in smoke.

Shihaung was terrified when told of the incident and given the piece of jade, he had it examined by his imperial treasurers and then finally admitted it was the same piece he had sacrificed to the Yangtze River in 219 B.C., almost a decade earlier.

This admission stunned the court because water was the guardian-element of the dynasty, and since now the water was returning his offering, it seemed all too likely that the gods and heavens had rejected the emperor.

Shihuang, quivering in the face of what he saw as this overwhelming heavenly disfavour, was suddenly unable to use his armies to answer inauspicious signs. Perhaps he finally realized he was failing and, perhaps, foresaw his own death.

Omens and portents were taken seriously in Shihuang's time and it was believed that unusual phenomena constituted a warning to the ruler to reform, since "Good deeds produce things of a good nature and foul deeds summon foul events." Thus, Heaven produced portents like eclipses, comets, and meteors, while Earth produced omens like floods, earthquakes, plagues of insects, and even the birth of strange animals such as two-headed dogs.

Like Shihuang, subsequent Chinese Emperors employed great numbers of astronomers to monitor these happenings, and as a result China has produced the most accurate and complete record of astral phenomena in human history.

In 132 A.D., a Chinese inventor fashioned the world's first seismograph for the detection of earthquakes!

The gods in the heavens began to show their disfavour to Shihuang's reign at the end of his life. This stone rubbing shows supernatural beings in their domain above the clouds. In Chinese art, the cloud scroll motif generally signifies the divine.

Shihuang's Final Tour

CLOSE TO DESPERATION, the First Emperor now turned to his new army of oracles and astronomers. No satisfactory solution was recorded about the jade message, but Shihuang, guided in part by divination from magicians desperate to please the emperor, decided the time was auspicious for travel. And so, on November 1, ignoring the approaching winter, he set forth on what would become his final tour in 211 B.C.

Summarily ordering Li Si to accompany him, he took a southerly route to the sea, perhaps to revitalize his reign through the guardian element of water. The entourage also included his newly-favored son Hu Hai, who had impetuously asked to be included in the party. Concubines and eunuchs were also part of the royal entourage, including the most powerful of the eunuchs, Zhao Gao, who was officially in charge of dispatching any messages or decrees which the emperor wished to send back to the capital.

This tour, doomed to be his final trek across his beloved land, was fuelled again by the First Emperor's search for immortality. Depressed by omens, concerned about his own actions and feeling betrayed by his subjects, Shihuang felt an even greater urgency than before.

He was not yet fifty but his physical condition was probably poor – he was worn down by stress, by his agitated mental state and by the growing burden of managing an empire and deploying an army of increasingly rebellious workers. His refusal to delegate any authority whatsoever added to an already crushing work-load.

Shihuang remained obsessed with his search for the elusive secret of immortality. His magicians constantly failed to find the right herbs despite forays throughout the land and the sea, but Shihuang was so convinced that success was just around the corner that he kept full-time alchemists at court working constantly to synthesize the sacred herbs.

There are also indications that he tested some of the concoctions they created, drinking potions which contained such toxic elements as compounds of mercury and phosphorous. We can only conjecture as to the possible effects upon his health and wonder if the First Emperor might not have been slowly poisoning himself in his search for immortality.

One can imagine, then, the mental and physical state of the First Emperor as he made his last tour. Ailing and desperate, he ascended the high mountains to make sacrifices, and, for the first time in his life, paid obeisance to the sage-kings of antiquity. Never before had Shihuang acknowledged the power of any ancestors but his own, but with these rituals he was trying to protect his own soul and guarantee for himself a place among the kings who had trod and conquered the lands before him.

He usually climbed to the tops of the mountains on his own and, as he stood in silence before the burial mounds of the ancient kings, what thoughts, we wonder, passed through his mind, at this, the end of his life.

His first sacrifice was to Shun, a figure much admired by the Confucians, and it was made at a site never visited by him before. The second was made to Yu The Great, a king known for the beginnings of the irrigation and dike system that Shihuang had continued to construct during the unification period.

Here, close to Yu's tomb, Shihuang etched the last of his inscriptions, once again praising his own deeds and trying, perhaps desperately, to convince the long-dead Yu that his rule was worthy of preservation.

After these ritualistic acts, Shihuang turned northward to the coast, stopping to rest at Langyai where he called to account his magicians and asked for a report on the search for the immortals.

But the wily magicians had new excuses and told the emperor the elixir of immortality was to be found on Penglai, an island that was guarded by great herds of giant whales, variously described as sea serpents, monsters and creatures of the deep, depending on which history is read.

Shihuang was intrigued by this new explanation and the magicians told him they needed skilled archers to kill the sea beasts. Shihuang believed them and then, according to the *Shiji*, had a dream that he was locked in combat with a sea-god in human form.

Qin Shihuang sets out on his final tour, little knowing that his death was near.

The Death of Shihuang

THE FIRST EMPEROR now believed that in order to survive, he must first conquer a huge sea-god and then drink the elixir of eternal life.

In a final burst of passion, Shihuang immediately mobilized his huge entourage and searched the coastline for the sea-beasts, for a great school of giant fish. He ordered special crossbows fashioned to kill the monsters and fast boats constructed to master the swells and tides of the seas.

Finally, he located a school of great fish, probably whales, and shot and killed a huge specimen. Satisfied with his conquest and sure in his heart that the gods had been pacified, Shihuang set off on his long trek back to his capital of Xianyang. He had been gone almost eight months and it was now the time of sweet summer in the capital.

But the deities above were not happy and Shihuang, travelling in his special litter drawn by eight chargers, fell ill long before the capital was in sight. As he grew weaker, those around him knew his end was near. But they were so afraid of his mercurial anger that no one dared to raise the matter of arrangements for his funeral or for the succession, something which had long been a Chinese tradition when a ruler was about to die.

But Shihuang knew he was dying, and under his imperial seal he wrote a decree to his eldest son, Fu Su, who was stationed in disgrace at the Great Wall. The decree ordered him simply to meet the funeral cortege at Xianyang and to bury his father there. The implication, of course, was that Fu Su would be his successor.

Shihuang sent the letter to the eunuch, Zhao Gao, whose official position as Keeper of the Stables and Chariots, included the office which transmitted imperial missives. As Zhao Gao had plans of his own for the succession, the letter was never sent, and, in a grand irony, the last command of Shihuang was the first ever to be disobeyed. And shortly thereafter he died.

Aware of the potential for trouble within the discontented empire now that the emperor had died so far away from home, Li Si hit upon a bold plan. Enlisting the aid of Shihuang's son, Hu Hai, and his ex-tutor, Zhao Gao, along with other trusted eunuchs, he concealed the emperor's death in an elaborate charade whereby food was still delivered to Shihuang's covered chariot and decrees issued from it, as the procession returned to the capital.

During the return journey, Zhao Gao, who as Hu Hai's tutor had gained great influence over him, persuaded the weak prince as well as Li Si that if the sealed letter from the emperor was sent to Fu Su, all of them would be lost. They joined together in a plot to make Hu Hai the next emperor. They forged a letter to Fu Su in which his father supposedly reproached him for his earlier unfilial behavior and his failure to win new territory on the frontier. Along with the letter they sent a

This closed-in chariot was probably similar to the one which made possible the concealment of Qin Shihuang's death on the return to the capital.

sword with which he was ordered to kill himself. Fu Su, the most filial of sons, committed suicide, opening the way for Hu Hai's usurpation of the throne.

There was to be a final indignity for the First Emperor. The summer heat of the long journey home made it more and more difficult to conceal the fact that there was a corpse in the emperor's carriage. Li Si ordered a measure of highly odorous salt-fish placed in each carriage so that the occupants would

not notice any other smell. And so, in this manner, Shihuang was returned to his capital where, on the basis of yet another forged order, Hu Hai was proclaimed the Second Sovereign Emperor.

The Second Emperor of Qin

ZHAO GAO WAS CONFIDENT of his ability to dominate the new emperor because the young man had neither political experience nor the time to develop a core of official advisers. Although he had been raised in the palace he had not formed an agenda or plan of action for the future. Hu Hai, himself, deciding that his inadequacies as a ruler would soon become evident, moved quickly to eliminate all possible rivals. His first act as Second Emperor was to have both a number of his father's ministers and his other sons – his own brothers and half-brothers – executed. So frightened was he of plots against his throne, that even his sisters, who could scarcely constitute a threat, were killed.

One brother of Hu Hai was so terrified that he asked the Second Emperor for money to pay for his own burial in the tomb of Shihuang. He had decided it was better to follow his father to the grave than to wait for an ignominious death. The request was granted.

There was further slaughter among the palace guards and army in order to remove all possible dissidents and then Li Si was subtly removed from his relationship with the throne. The writing was on the wall as far as the Grand Councillor was concerned and the *Shiji* records that Hu Hai refused to grant audiences with Li Si and "made reproving inquiries" about all of his activities.

Two years later, in 208 B.C., Zhao Gao was to engineer Li Si's disgrace and death. Until his death Li Si continued to offer counsel but was seldom heeded and meanwhile Zhao Gao convinced the Second Emperor to withdraw to the inner palace and allow him and his coterie to direct the affairs of state.

Once Zhao Gao had manoeuvered Li Si out of the corridors of power, it was the beginning of the end for the young emperor. Even though Shihuang had proclaimed that his proud dynasty would last for "endless generations," Hu Hai would rule for barely two years and his successor, Zi Ying, for less than two months.

So complete was the collapse of the empire that the Third Emperor of Qin, Zi Ying, surrendered to a rebel army in 206 B.C. wearing a cord around his neck and driving a plain carriage with white horses, to show his humility and acceptance of defeat.

Hu Hai is remembered for one major act – the completion of his father's tomb at Mount Li. Regardless of his weakness, shortcomings and lack of vision, Hu Hai was rigid in his obedience to what he saw as the will of his dead father, regardless of the cost.

When the tomb was complete, Hu Hai had already begun to question his future: *"The leading ministers question my policies, the officials hold [too] much power, and the [remaining] princes are determined to contest my authority. What shall I do?"*

Zhao Gao had a simple solution – an inspection tour that would become in essence an execution march. False crimes would be discovered against ministers and officials, questionable army officers would be beheaded, and all those whom Hu Hai feared would disappear.

"This is not the time for gentleness," said Zhao Gao. *"Strength is required. I beg you to act swiftly before these officials have time to plot, so that as a wise ruler you win over the rest of your subjects, raising up the lowly, enriching the poor and making the distant close. Then high and low will rally to your cause and the Empire will be secure."*

Hu Hai followed this advice and conducted a royal purge – a purge that sparked a rebellion among the Blackhaired people that would further hasten the downfall of the already weakened Qin empire.

All imperial decrees had to bear the seal of the emperor. Large, heavy, and carved from jade, Qin Shihuang's seal was lost in the centuries following his death.

Zhao Gao, the crafty eunuch who had been the tutor of Shihuang's weak son, Hu Hai, altered the First Emperor's true will so that his ex-pupil would become the Second Emperor.

The Tomb of Shihuang

THE TOMB IN WHICH HU HAI buried his father is one of the wonders of the world. More than 700,000 men were commissioned to build it, and when they were finally finished, Hu Hai ordered many of them entombed with his father, Shihuang, so that they would never be able to reveal its secrets to grave-robbers. He also sent the childless concubines of the First Emperor into the mausoleum to be buried with their former ruler. It would be the last time that such a hideous act would ever take place in China.

We cannot be sure when the construction on the tomb was begun, though some scholars believe the plans for it were made as early as 246 B.C. when Shihuang became King of Qin. Others say that is was not until 212 B.C. that actual work on the site began.

What lies within the tomb is still unknown, but the *Shiji* describes its grand concept:

"And the First Emperor was buried at Mount Li.

"From the time he first came to the throne, Shihuang had begun the excavation and building at Mount Li, and when he had gathered into his hands the whole empire, more than 700,000 workers were sent to the site to toil.

"Through three underground springs they dug, and they poured molten bronze to make the outer coffin and to make the models of the palaces, pavilions and government offices with which the tomb was filled.

"And there were marvelous tools and precious jewels and rare objects brought from afar. Artisans were ordered to fashion crossbows as traps so that any grave-robbers would meet sudden death.

"Using quicksilver, they made the hundred rivers of the land, the Yellow and the Yangtse, and the wide sea, and machines kept the waters in motion. The constellations of the heavens were reproduced above and the regions of the earth below.

We have talked at length of the tomb of Shihuang, but other finds from the Qin and Han dynasties have also contributed much to our understanding of Chinese culture.

These tombs were mainly of prominent and wealthy members of society. Because belief in the after-life was strong, the tombs have rich furnishings including jade and bronze, lacquer vessels, talismans, musical instruments and comments, either written on wooden or bamboo strips or on silk.

Other necessities of everyday life in China circa 200 B.C. included lamps, dishes, plates, weapons and exquisite boxes of lacquer. There were also clothes, food, drink and money.

The Han tombs, like that of Shihuang, contain carriages, boats, millstones or miniature farmyards complete with pigs. The body of the deceased was preserved carefully thanks to the techniques of the undertakers and the nature of the soil.

The hill-like mound of Qin Shihuang's tomb blends in naturally with the Xi'an countryside.

"Torches were made of whale oil to burn for a long time. Concubines without sons were ordered to follow the emperor in death and of the artisans and workers, not one was allowed to emerge alive.

"Vegetation was planted so that it appeared to be a mountain."

This, then, was his tomb, complete with replicas of his palaces and a silent clay army rigidly arrayed before it in battle formation. It was a monument to his majesty and a dark reminder of the suffering of his people.

Probably no other ruler of China created a memorial of this magnitude. And the tomb was not just as the *Shiji* described it – it was much, much more. Excavations which began in 1974 show that the *Shiji* description is inadequate.

To begin, the site is huge – the earthen mound covering the mausoleum is about 45 metres high, somewhat less than half the height recorded in the third century A.D. and a fact easily explained by erosion. The total circumference of the tomb is eight miles.

And its exterior is far more elaborate than the *Shiji* description. There were gardens, four gates leading to the enclosures, corner towers, a sacrificial palace, and in all likelihood, residences for priests and guards.

Literary evidence suggests the tomb has twice been opened, first by the troops of the rebels in 207 B.C. in a search for weapons, and then 700 years later when it was plundered. Until the excavations are completed, we will not know what depredations have been done to it.

The inner tomb of Shihuang has not yet been opened as Chinese archaeologists painstakingly sift by hand through the outer pits and courtyards. So far, they have uncovered only the incredible terracotta army of Shihuang.

The Fall of Qin

THE FIRST CIVIL DISOBEDIENCE against the rule of the Qin empire came about because a young farmhand was threatened with death for disobedience. This act, coupled with the years of increasing concern over the rule from the palace, turned into an insurrection with thousands of peasants, many of whom had military training, rising against the laws and officials of Qin.

Hu Hai, without the counsel of most of the wise generals of Shihuang, decided to stamp out the uprising by raising an army of convicts and pulling back troops from other construction duties. The convict army succeeded in putting down the peasants, but it was more the act of stamping on a spark, than of putting out a fire.

More and more peasant uprisings were reported, rebel leaders sprouted everywhere and Hu Hai, blindly following Zhao Gao's advice, retired to the luxury of the inner palace at Xianyang, guarded by a special garrison of 50,000 hand-picked fighters.

Li Si and the old guard of Shihuang's generals begged the young Second Emperor to do something about the rebellions, warning of brigands and reminding him that the imperial army of convicts had not wiped out the uprising.

But Hu Hai accused these loyal subjects of his father of incompetence and told them *"you are unfit for office."* Two generals committed suicide and Li Si was forced to endure the "five tortures," before his execution.

With that act, the wolves were unleashed and ambitious men outside the guarded passes of Qin saw their chance to bring down the Qin regime.

One such leader was Xiang Yü who moved boldly to take over a commandery in the lower Yangtze valley and decapitate the governor. He had been a loyal follower of Shihuang and hated his weak son Hu Hai. And he was a legendary warrior, so strong it was said, that he could lift a great bronze cauldron above his head.

His success in the Yangtze brought more and more disgrun-

The collapse of the Qin empire followed swiftly on the heels of the First Emperor's death.

tled peasants to his cause and in 207 B.C., the rebel army crossed the Yellow River and met the forces of Hu Hai. Xiang Yü forced his men to sink their boats, smash their canteens and throw away their food. Victory was the only possibility, and it was achieved.

This defeat spread discontent and dissension through the main Qin army and Xiang Yü took advantage of it, mounting a surprise attack on the main force by night at the Wei River Valley. The *Shiji* says 200,000 were butchered and the military power of Qin was irrevocably ended.

The Second Emperor was disgraced and the eunuch Zhao Gao wasted no time in turning the court against him, framing him for a murder and so humiliating him that the confused and weak Hu Hai finally killed himself.

Zhao Gao then engineered the succession of Zi Ying, a nephew of Shihuang, but the Third Emperor only sat on the throne for 46 days before abjectly surrendering to the rebels. Zhao Gao tried to fit the imperial seal to his own belt, but no official would accept his usurpation and the fall of Qin was complete. The eunuch was killed, and soon afterwards, a new dynasty, the Han, was proclaimed. It would hold sway for almost 400 years.

The guardian army mired in the earth is a tangible reminder of the fallen glory of the Qin.

The rebel Xiang Yu.

The Rise of the Han Dynasty

THE QIN DYNASTY was brought to a formal end not by the arrogant warrior Xiang Yü, but by a coarse peasant who rose through the ranks of another rebel force to become the founder and first ruler of the Han dynasty.

He is known to history as Gaozu, or "High Progenitor", a name given him after his death. He was a native of Central China who, like Xiang Yü, had thrown off the yoke of servitude and killed the Qin magistrate of his home area. He then quickly raised a force of convicts and peasants and threw his support behind the King of Chu who was also fighting against the embattled Qin empire.

Gaozu rose quickly, history tells us, and soon led his own large force which succeeded in penetrating the heart of the Qin stronghold in the Wei River Valley. It was he who accepted the formal surrender of the Third Qin Emperor, Zi Ying, and found himself in command of the imperial capital of Xianyang. The dynasty founded by Shihuang came to an end in the tenth month, 206 B.C. It had lasted for only fifteen years.

But Gaozu did not pillage or destroy, but simply awaited orders from the King of Chu, his commander. However Xiang Yü arrived first, and had the last emperor of Qin murdered, the palaces set on fire, and even allowed his troops to pillage the mausoleum of Shihuang.

Xiang Yü had a master plan of his own – to form a confederacy of states with himself as head, and to eliminate any possible opposition, he had the King of Chu assassinated, and attempted to "buy off" Gaozu by awarding to him the mountainous territory known as Han.

That set the stage for a final battle for mastery between the two leaders. Gaozu took the initiative by defeating three newly-declared kings and advancing to Xiang Yü's base.

However, he was soundly defeated by Xiang Yü's forces and it was only thanks to a storm that he was able to make his escape with a handful of cavalry. But the wily Gaozu was not yet finished. He retired to the east and was able to rebuild his support there and establish a new base of operations.

Xiang Yü, outraged, marched again against his hated adversary and lay siege to his base. Gaozu was defeated again and barely escaped with his life. But Xiang Yü still could not control eastern China – Gaozu's stronghold – and finally, in 203 B.C., confronted him and offered to settle the future of China by single combat.

Gaozu, who by now had raised his third army, demanded a full trial of military strength. Instead, however, they reached a formal agreement to divide China between them, with Gaozu as Lord of Han and Xiang Yü as Lord of Chu.

Gaozu, fine strategist that he was, wasted no time in breaking the agreement. Realizing that his rival's army was exhausted, he mounted one final attack, and succeeded in circling the demoralized force. Most surrendered.

The *Shiji* tells us that Xiang Yü escaped, but was left with only twenty-eight followers and, with a last great show of courage, committed suicide.

Gaozu had used warfare to gain an empire, ironically following the same path Shihuang had trodden forty years earlier. And, in, 202 B.C., he took the title of emperor, which had been created by Shihuang.

Gaozu, the peasant leader who established four hundred years of Han rule.

In spite of Qin Shihuang's Great Wall, the nomads remained a constant threat, and Han dynasty tombs were often built with watchtowers.

TEN THOUSAND GENERATIONS

The Legacy of Qin Shihuang

The Moral Failure of the Qin Dynasty

ALTHOUGH THE LACK OF LEADERSHIP was the most obvious and dramatic cause of the Qin Dynasty's failure to survive for long after the death of the First Emperor, there were other factors of equal importance. It is true that power so heavily concentrated needed strong hands to hold it, and the Second Emperor was not just inexperienced, and ill-prepared for the task, but he was also a fool and something of a lazy debauchee. He sacrificed to the ambitions of a cunning eunuch, the life of the one man, Li Si, who might have helped him, and to his administration generally, one is tempted to apply the charge that he "fiddled while China burned."

When we regard his rule, we also see that the Second Emperor disregarded one of the three central Legalist tenets: the use of "methods" to manipulate his ministers in such a way that none ever gained dominance over him. But still, whatever imbalance this created, it need not have been fatal, since, theoretically, the universal rule of law should have maintained order among the masses. In pure Legalism, and as Zhao Gao advised the Second Emperor, "[If you] make the laws more severe, and the punishments heavier ... appoint [only] those with whom you are close and surround yourself with people you trust ... [then] what is harmful will disappear and evil plots will be cut short ... Your Majesty may than recline peacefully on His high pillow, giving free rein to his desires, and enjoying what gives him pleasure."

Shihuang, realizing that the theory was flawed, had been shrewd enough to change and adapt. His son was not.

Nonetheless, the speed with which the Qin Dynasty collapsed suggests that the discontent was deeper, more widespread, and of longer-standing than can be explained by mere failure within the Second Emperor's palace and court. And several explanations have been advanced.

In the traditional view, the fall of the Qin dynasty was caused by its moral failure. It was a harsh and cruel reign that existed for the rulers, not for all the people. The root of this view lies in the famous essay of Jia Yi (201-169 B.C.) called "The Sins of Qin," which the historian Sima Qian considered so excellent that he appended it *in toto* to Shihuang's annals in the *Shiji*. Thus, every scholar studying Shihuang's life was exposed to it. It reads, in part:

... And then there came the First Emperor to carry on the great achievements of six generations [of his ancestors]. Cracking his long whip, he drove the whole world before him ... He climbed to the highest position and extended his sway over the six directions, scourging the world with his rod, and shaking the four seas with his power ... Then, he discarded the ways of the former kings and burned the writings of the "Hundred Schools" in order to keep his people mired in ignorance. He tore down the great fortifications of the states, executed their powerful leaders, collected all the arms of the Empire, and had them brought to his capital at Xianyang ... all this in order to weaken the people of the Empire ... He garrisoned each strategic point with expert generals and skilful bowmen and placed his trusted officials and well-trained soldiers where they could protect the land with their weapons and question all who passed back and forth ... He believed deep within his heart that ... he had built a dynasty that would be enjoyed by his descendents for ten-thousand generations.

And for a while after the death of the First Emperor, the memory of his strength continued to over-awe the common people ...

But only for a short while.

振長策而御宇內吞
二周而亡諸侯履至
尊而制六合執棰拊
以鞭笞天下威振四

This selection from the famous essay *"The Sins of Qin"* is written in the calligraphic style of Jia Yi's time.

An Unpopular Reign

WHEN WE CONSIDER THE MAGNIFICENCE of the Imperial Qin Dynasty – the fact that Qin Shihuang had become the absolute master of a grand empire, it seems hard to believe that his ancestral temples could be toppled so quickly by a single commoner. And yet the Second Qin Emperor ruled for only three years and his successor for less than two months. And when the days of this great dynasty had ended, there were few who regretted its fall, and many who applauded.

Why?

According to one theory there were two reasons: The Qin Dynasty failed to rule with humanity and righteousness, and it also failed to realize that there are two kinds of power: One that seizes by force, and the other that retains what has been seized – and these two kinds of power are not one and the same.

There is, at least, a partial truth in this view, and we need look no farther than Shihuang's huge conscriptions of labour for the Great Wall and the palaces at Xianyang to understand his people's disaffection for his rule. Neither the privileged classes – the former nobility, the scholars and wealthy merchants – nor the peasantry could prosper under his rule, and it may be significant that the First Emperor's later critics came from the privileged Confucian scholars who must have shud-

△
▷ *The Blackhaired people suffered severely under the harsh rule of Qin Shihuang.*

dered to think of what their own fates might have been under his rule. Although absolute rulers are not usually noted for either morality or benevolence, and Shihuang was no different in these respects from many of the emperors who would later follow him, because he was the First Emperor, he had become the exemplar. He would be either emulated or rejected by those who followed him, and his critics hoped fervently that their writings would dissuade future emperors from the path Shihuang had taken.

Another explanation for the fall of Qin is also related to the fact of Shihuang being "first." Although never denying the intellect of Shihuang, traditional historians have castigated him for failing to learn from history. In his rush to be an innovator, to be the first in all things, they suggest that he both failed to emulate the goodness of the sages of the past and to avoid the harsh government which had destroyed so many earlier rulers. Although we may or may not agree, we can scarcely argue with the same historians' depiction of the Second Emperor as a man both intellectually and morally blind. Several historians, however, depict the entire Qin dynasty as anti-intellectual, using its book-burning and its pogrom of the scholars as proof. But as we have tried to show, Shihuang directed his intellect to the realities of statecraft in all its manifestations, and to the study of spiritual and sacred matters. Neither statemanship

nor religion can be regarded as frivolous or anti-intellectual interests! Nor did he ever discourage anyone from the study of war, agriculture or medicine. And, it must be remembered, he attempted to preserve copies of the burned books in the Imperial Library for the use of scholars.

But the dramatic impact of the book-burning and its aftermath must have certainly alienated the scholars, and perhaps all of the educated classes during the last years of the dynasty.

Another explanation for the fall of the dynasty concerns the other alienated groups who lived under Shihuang's rule. The social structure of China in the Qin dynasty is still something of a mystery, but as in all societies, there must have been group identification and group interest. What happened to the dispossessed royalty and nobility of the conquered states when they were transported to Xianyang? Could they be expected to support Shihuang? And what about the hundreds of thousands of conscripted labourers, dispossessed colonists, and convicted criminals, who were often mutilated or even castrated, and condemned to forced labour? Or the merchants, officially despised and sometimes transported to new colonies or to slavery on the Great Wall?

There must have been a deep pool of resentment, even hatred for Shihuang, or the early rebels against the regime would not have found so much support!

Too Much, Too Soon

A FOURTH EXPLANATION FOR THE FALL is simply that of over-ambition – the dynasty attempted to do too much, too fast. In the third-century B.C., China may well have been the most advanced of contemporary human civilizations, but its geographical size was enormous, its communications primitive, and its populace illiterate. The changes brought about by Shihuang were imposed from above and how deeply they permeated through the society, we can only conjecture. So massive was his projected transformation that it is inconceivable that it could be totally absorbed and assimilated by the people under him during the single decade of his rule. And the impatience he showed in implementing his vision must surely have caused pockets of disaffection in certain quarters.

It is clear that Shihuang was not content to wait even a decade for this transformation. The long stone inscription he erected on Mount Langyai in 218 B.C. was set up to exalt the power of his dynasty only three years after its establishment, and, according to the *Shiji*, to "make manifest his will."

A new age has been inaugurated by the [First] Emperor; Laws and measures have been made right . . .
Agriculture, the root occupation, is encouraged, and all secondary pursuits discouraged . . .
Tools and measures are of uniform standard . . .
The written script is everywhere the same . . .
Local customs have been regulated . . .
Irrigation ditches have been made and the farmlands divided . . .
The Emperor makes [new] laws, leaving nothing unclear, and telling his people the prohibitions.
The magistrates know their duties and smoothly is the work of the government carried out . . .
The tasks [of the farmer] are done in due season, and all things grow and prosper.
The people know peace and have laid down their armour and their weapons . . .
The realm of the Emperor
Extends to the lands of the desert,
And South to where the dwellings face north;
East to the Eastern Oceans,

Stelae which Shihuang inscribed on his tours demonstrate his desire for the rapid transformation of the world as he knew it.

And North to beyond the lands of Daxia . . .
His compassion bathes even the beasts of the field,
All living things benefit from his virtue,
And dwell quietly in tranquility, at home!

However, few of Shihuang's subjects were ever given that chance.

Think of a magistrate who is forced to learn immediately, hundreds of new laws; a farmer, suddenly conscripted to fight in the cold and remote north; a mother bidding goodbye to a son called that very day to labour at the capital. Think of the chaos when taxes were raised without notice or explanation, or when the First Emperor was touring an area and his entourage needed the grain which every family had so carefully stored for the winter. And on, and on and on.

All of these "small" dislocations were part of Shihuang's larger vision and perhaps, even of a greater good for the state. But it may be the case that from the beginning, the resources of Shihuang were overextended. He overestimated his powers; and his only hope, one which became more and more evident to him in the last years of his life, was that he would live forever. But ordinary people did not have so long, and their lives were being made even shorter and more unhappy by the emperor who had promised them peace.

The time of Qin Shihuang was one in which the Chinese had already developed a high degree of skill in bronze casting and jade carving, to name but two achievements. This jade dragon, with the smooth curves of its outline and low relief decoration, illustrate this. Jade was the hardest substance known to the Chinese at that time, and the stone was fashioned through grinding and wearing away with an abrasive rather than through cutting.

The Legacy Rejected

THE *CAMBRIDGE HISTORY OF CHINA*, the most recent scholarly study of the Qin dynasty and of the works of Shihuang, concludes with the judgment that whether or not one admired Shihuang's achievement, it had to be recognized as so great a transformation of the face of China that it deserved the name "revolution" even though it had been imposed by the ruler, rather than forced by the populace. Indeed, the study concludes, "it was China's only real revolution until the present century."

This judgement strikes us as a true one.

We do not know how tightly Shihuang was able to fasten his "revolution" upon China in his own time, but we do know that he left a legacy which has never been surpassed.

For two thousand years, the most populous people on the face of the earth lived their lives and laboured at their work, bore their children and buried their dead, in the world Shihuang had created. Ironically, the man whose burning of the books was a public rejection of the past, himself became a figure whose life was later used by historians as an object lesson for all future generations of Chinese.

There were two faces to his legacy, and the first was a rejection of all the First Emperor had stood for.

The founder of the next dynasty, the Han, was a man of peasant origin, known to history by his posthumous "temple name" of Gaozu or "lofty progenitor." He was, according to the sources, a man with a "dragon forehead," a large nose and a full beard, and a sensualist, fond of women and wine. It is said that on his left thigh he had seventy-two moles – a number considered a mystical one because the multiplication of the two highest male and female numbers (9×8), came to this total and combined with the Five Elements (5×72), came to the number of days in the Chinese year. But whatever signs of greatness lay upon him, he was not an educated man and had no grand scheme for the dynasty he founded. His aim was simply to overthrow the Qin dynasty and all that it had meant.

It is of great significance that his very first act on entering the Qin capital in 206 B.C., even before the proclamation of his own dynasty, was the abolition of the Qin law code. This suggests that the code was the most unpopular feature of the dynasty, but perhaps not so much for its harshness as for its complexity. The code Han established was far more simple, specifying punishments as heavy as those of the Qin, but only for murder, injury and theft.

Only in the second month of 202 B.C. did Gaozu formerly declare himself *huangdi* or "Sovereign Emperor" of the long-lived Han dynasty, which was to endure, with a short inter-regnum, for four centuries. Like all of China's future emperors, he had no hesitation in using the title created by Shihuang, and in those early years, he even adopted most of the religious practices and ceremonials of the late Emperor. But he rapidly found that to give even lip service to anything which smacked of the previous regime was immensely unpopular. In 205 B.C., he had expressed a desire to continue as his own guardian element, the force of water, the guardian element of the Qin dynasty. The suggestion was greeted with horror, and in time, and after much debate, he was forced to accept the patronship of earth, being persuaded by the argument that earth soaks up, and so overcomes water.

But if Gaozu could not follow the philosophy of Legalism, which had, after all, unified "the world" after five centuries of division, where would he find a guiding ideology for his new dynasty?

Confucianism was the obvious alternative. It provided a blueprint for the humane and well-ordered state, but it would have no appeal for a rough-hewn peasant like Gaozu. With its high-flying idealism, its rich store of precedent and ancient lore, its insistence on education, on the niceties of etiquette and the virtuous example that should be set by the cultivated ruler, he must have seen it as an inappropriate solution for a man attempting to bring order out of the chaos of the Qin collapse.

One of the more vivid images of Gaozu in Chinese literature tells of him meeting with a group of Confucian scholars who are trying to persuade him to their point of view. After listening to their arguments, he expressed his own opinion. Seizing the high official cap of their spokesman, he stood before them all and urinated in it.

In the following Han dynasty, the Legalist tenets of Shihuang were cast aside. Here, an instructress teaches Confucian principles to court ladies.

The Legacy Accepted

AFTER THE REJECTION OF Qin's Legalism, and the Confucian scholars whose doctrines were as yet, imperfectly understood, there was but one alternative left. Taoism, and the whole amalgam of folk-belief which clustered around it seemed the answer to Gaozu.

The first half-century of Han rule was therefore dominated by the Taoist doctrine of *wei-wu-wei*, – "do nothing and nothing will not be done." For the only extended period in Chinese history, more than half a century, the emperors sat "with unruffled garments and folded hands." The rejection of Qin Shihuang's legacy allowed the Chinese people finally to rest.

During this period, the population increased, new land was opened, and commerce flourished. However, even though the state became more complex and the tasks of government more demanding, little was changed. Taxes remained far lower than they had been under Shihuang, and raids by the Xiongnu or Huns along the northern frontier became ever more persistent and were so successful that they threatened the capital, causing many to suggest that it be moved to a safer location in the east.

And in the year 141 B.C., there came to the throne in China another young man, still a teenager, who would turn out to be the real heir of Qin Shihuang and indeed, who ruled in so similar a fashion, that he could have been his later incarnation!

Known as the emperor, Han Wudi, he was to rule for a long time, until 87 B.C.; and under him, consolidation gave way to expansion: There were new laws and heavier taxes and great building schemes and military campaigns and the strict, sometimes harsh control of court and countryside which had marked Shihuang's career.

Like Shihuang, he was determined to rule the whole empire without irritant or distraction, and though the quasi-feudal principalities established by Gaozu were no direct threat, he determined to emasculate them. Thus, he made heavy and arbitrary financial demands on them, stripped the lords of their titles on the slightest pretext, and decreed that their domains be equally divided among all male heirs, so that they continually shrank in size. By the end of his long reign, their existence was more fictional than real.

Also like Shihuang, he was no real admirer of the merchant class, many of whom had amassed huge fortunes under the *laissez-faire* policies of the early Han rulers, since they were largely exempt from taxation. Wudi changed all that. He levied numerous taxes on mercantile activity, forbade merchants to own farmland by the foreclosure of mortgages, and established state monopolies on salt, iron and even liquor, so that these lucrative trades enriched the throne, rather than falling into private hands.

The name "Wudi" in Chinese means the "Martial Emperor," and his title was well-deserved. If anything, his military successes exceeded those of Shihuang. He subdued renegade Chinese states in the far south and southeast between 111-109 B.C., and at the same time extended Chinese control over Manchuria and the Korean peninsula. His greatest triumphs, however, came against the Xiongnu, or Huns, who had been activated by Shihuang's aggressive policies. Beginning in 133 B.C., he began to direct the energies of his people against them for almost two decades until he controlled most of Inner Mongolia and Chinese Turkestan. He sent, it is said, 700,000 Chinese to farm and colonize the area, just as Shihuang had done in other border regions.

And like the First Emperor, he was deeply interested in the sacred, the occult and the quest for immortality. He performed, throughout his reign, many of the same sacrifices as Shihuang on Mount Tai, sent his generals in 102 B.C. in search for the famous "blood-sweating horses" of Fergana. Again, just as the First Emperor had, he surrounded himself with magicians who promised, but failed, to synthesize the magic elixir or obtain it from the Eastern Isles.

An even more active seeker of immortality than Shihuang, Han Wudi was to ensure that the positive side of the First Emperor's legacy endured up till the twentieth century in China.

Han Wudi was dominated by his mother, the Empress Dowager, in the early years of his reign. Not only did she put to death those tutors who taught her son what she regarded as the "wrong" teachings, but she also placed many members of her own family in positions of power. He made no protest, for the Chinese tenets of filial piety demanded that a son obey his mother.

A good deal of Chinese political history, therefore, was controlled not by the emperors, but by their widowed mothers.

Wudi's solution to this problem was a death-bed decree that his widow be put to death so that she could not influence her son, the new emperor.

Regrettably, there were later emperors who also followed his example.

The standardization of weights, measures and coinage helped to forge a true unity of the Chinese people. Just as the coins became recognizable as belonging to one nation, so too did the Chinese people.

The Enduring Legacy

IT WAS THE IDEA of unity that was Shihuang's most positive legacy to China. The early Han rulers had restored a much scaled-down version of feudalism, complete with noble titles and feoffdoms for the early supporters of the regime and the sons of the early emperors. But conscious of the danger of separatism, they had gradually reduced the powers of the kingdoms, and even provoked seven kings to rebellion in 154 B.C. After the suppression of this uprising, steps were taken to ensure that it never happened again, and Wudi carried out a number of administrative measures, most notably in 108 B.C., which gave him a degree of centralized power in every sense equal to what Shihuang had enjoyed. By the end of the dynasty, around 220 A.D., the people of China thought only in terms of a unified, centralized empire. Never again would any dynasty seek seriously to re-introduce feudalism.

Secondly, the Han rulers, after the first period of *laissez-faire* government, began to employ one after the other, the organizing principles initiated under Shihuang. The systems of provincial administration, taxes and labour services, universal miliary conscription and other aspects of the Qin order were modified, usually in the direction of less harshness, but there is no question that the policies of Qin Shihuang were followed as the model.

A third and positive part of Shihuang's legacy was the Imperial system of government. The manner in which the position of emperor evolved in the first fifty years of the Han is a complex story, and need not be told here. Suffice it to say that Wudi insisted upon and received every prerogative which Shihuang had demanded. He also meted out harsh punishment to every official who failed him or whose criticism was too trenchant, and by the end of Wudi's long reign, the position

of emperor had been defined very much in Shihuang's terms, and was to change very little thereafter. It is interesting to note that Sima Qian, the author of the *Shiji*, had been castrated by Wudi for his outspokenness, and some scholars believe that his unfavourable historical treatment of Qin Shihuang was, in fact, a veiled criticism of his own emperor!

Fourthly, within a decade of Shihuang's death, and in spite of the widespread criticism of his laws, the Han dynasty came to the realization that the short, simplistic legal code of Gaozu was ineffective. Hence, in 200 B.C., a new code was issued

which actually enlarged the six-chapter Qin code by three chapters, and as far as we can tell, made little change in the nature of criminal punishment. Subsequent emperors, however, modified this, "Confucianizing" the law with the abolition of the harsher penalties, and although officials were still subject to stern punishment for any malfeasance on their part, they were also allowed special privileges which set them apart from the common herd. Shihuang's legacy was the example for later ages of a detailed, regular nationwide system of laws which throughout history contributed to a high degree of social order both in court and the countryside.

Little more need be said of the standardization of such things as weights and measures, of currency and the writing system. Changes occurred in later times, but they were minor in nature and the principle of a single unifying standard for the whole country was never again challenged. Shihuang's roads endured for some centuries, and though gradually they fell into disrepair as economic conditions changed and water transport gained in importance, they had done their work. His major canals, of course, exist to the present day.

A Symbol for the Ages

QIN SHIHUANG'S LEGACY of the Great Wall cannot be overestimated. Its practical value as a barrier to invasion has been much debated, but most scholars agree that when properly-manned, it was fairly effective. If it could never stop the full-scale nomadic invasions which so often placed parts of north China, and indeed, sometimes the whole country, under "barbarian" rule in later times, it did effectively delay and discourage smaller-scale raids which could have prevented Chinese settlement in the north and northwest and made the peasants' life there a misery.

But far more importantly, the Wall defined the Chinese identity, dividing symbolically, the civilized "within" from the uncivilized "without." It marked the territory which emperors from Shihuang onward needed to rule firmly, directly and benevolently to be considered legitimate as "Sons of Heaven." What lay outside the Wall was of marginal interest, perceived only in terms of potential threat, and China, therefore, has been one of the least imperialistic of nations throughout her long history. By unifying and extending all the existing walls, Qin Shihuang created a Long Wall which gave China a defined border, and one which satisfied most of his successors. Only a very few of the most ambitious emperors ever sent their troops beyond it in search of conquest.

And so, through the ages it served the cause of peace rather than of war. It was one of Shihuang's greatest gifts to later generations of the "Blackhaired people."

And ironically, the long-term legacy of the "burning of the books" turned out to be a positive one. The symbol of all that was harsh and philistine about the Qin dynasty, the destruction of the empire's books impressed on later generations the value of their heritage, and the study of the classical tradition in China far exceeds that of any other civilization. In every age of Chinese history, education began with the carefully reconstructed books which Shihuang had burned. So powerful have books always been considered in China, that their importance, even in our own time, has led to the persecution of scholars who have often become martyrs of the written word. Shihuang's attempted destruction of the works of China's greatest philosophers – men who had contemplated the human condition and who had offered their own modest guidelines for a good life – made later generations determine to die, if need be, rather than once again lose their written history. What Shihuang had tried to destroy, he preserved forever.

Who was he, and what was he, this First Emperor of China?

Although there are no clear anwers, he was, unquestionably, a great man. If sometimes flawed, and often wrong he did create a country, China, which has made enormous contributions to the science and culture of the world's civilizations.

It is as both a symbol and an exemplar, that Qin Shihuang lives on in today's China. His deeds live just as surely as 7,000 terracotta soldiers stand guard over his last resting-place.

BACKGROUND

The Background of the Book and Film

THE STORY BEHIND THE FILM of THE FIRST EMPEROR OF CHINA, and the book which was created as a result of it, is unique. It marks the first time the National Film Board of Canada and the People's Republic of China have collaborated on a movie shot in the wide-screen Imax format.

The almost $7 million film, to open June 27, 1989, at a gala at the new Canadian Museum of Civilization in Ottawa and later to be shown in museum theatres across North America, is the realization of a dream for veteran director Tony Ianzelo of the National Film Board.

With 23 documentaries to his credit, including 4 films about China, Ianzelo conceived the idea for THE FIRST EMPEROR OF CHINA after a visit to the country nine years ago. He proposed filming a documentary about Shihuang's terracotta army of 7,000 life-size figures buried with the Emperor in his huge mausoleum in 210 B.C.

Ianzelo opened discussions with the China Xi'an Film Studio and with the help of co-producers Barrie Howells and Margaret Wong, years of negotiations were finally concluded. In 1987, a new round of careful talks was begun to assure Chinese cultural experts that its terracotta treasures would be carefully respected in the film which had now been broadened to a 40-minute docudrama on the life and achievements of Shihuang.

A Chinese co-director, Liù Hao Xue, was appointed to work with Ianzelo and THE FIRST EMPEROR OF CHINA marks the first time he has worked on a film that had entirely synchronized sound. Finally, a NFB crew under Ianzelo journeyed to China to film, on location, the story of Shihuang, an incredible history of the god-like ruler who is almost unknown to the Western world.

Full co-operation was extended by the Chinese ministry of culture in Beijing and the Chinese Embassy in Ottawa, Canada, which were eager to collaborate on an Imax production, a 70 mm process that uses screens 30 metres wide by 23 metres high.

Filming began in China's Shaanxi Province on October 30, 1988, and ended on February 13, 1989. It was the first time, a foreign film board had shot actual footage at the archaeological dig at Shihuang's huge eight-mile round tomb.

THE FIRST EMPEROR OF CHINA is the largest project in the history of the Xi'an Studio and at peak production, more than 1,100 were employed behind the scenes. A total of 368 Chinese and 10 Canadians worked on location on the film including 39 costume designers, 35 makeup artists, 30 prop builders, 22 art designers, 40 lighting technicians and 30 horse trainers.

There were 11 studio sets and 20 major locations shot and a royal palace, seven-storeys-high, was built for the film. Props and costumes were made at 37 different factories and one took an entire month just to make the silk for the costumes.

The 40-minute movie used 1,600 extras for the epic battle scenes, 180 horses and 30 battle chariots, each carefully built to replicate the war wagons of Shihuang (246-210 B.C.). More than 700 musicians were assembled in front of the palace in one shot alone.

A total of 1,000 suits of armor were made and 3,200 pairs of shoes and boots were also painstakingly recreated. More than 3,200 weapons were used as props including 200 cross-bows, the weapons used by Shihuang's vast armies of 600,000 to conquer the Warring States of China.

This book, THE FIRST EMPEROR OF CHINA, was created and developed in close co-operation with Colin Neale, executive producer, of the National Film Board, during the final stages of the shooting and editing of the film.

Further Reading

THIS IS A WORK designed for the general reader, and as such, utilizes a good deal of published research.

For several reasons, the authors have avoided the use of footnotes, but would like in this short essay, to acknowledge those who have gone before them and at the same time, to provide the interested reader with the opportunity for further exploration.

The principal source for the study of Qin Shihuang and his dynasty is, of course, the *Shiji*. This lengthy work has never been fully translated, but the great French Sinologist, E. Chavannes has provided a nearly complete translation in five volumes, entitled *Les mémoires historiques de Se-Ma Ts'ien*. While most translations were made directly from the Chinese, we have relied heavily on the most recent edition of this work, from E.J. Brill (Leiden, 1967). In English, Hsien-yi and Gladys Yang have translated several sections of the *Shiji*, including the annals of Shihuang, in *Records of the Historian*, (Hong Kong, 1974); and B. Watson, in *Records of the Grand Historian of China*, (New York, 1961), and *Records of the Historian* (New York, 1965) has translated the biographies of many other figures of the period.

Professor D. Bodde has long been interested in the Qin period and has produced three useful works. The earliest, *China's First Unifier* (Leiden, 1938), propounds the thesis that Li Si was the real unifier of China and was responsible for most of Shihuang's policies. In *Statesman, Patriot, and General* (New Haven, 1940), he provides carefully annotated biographies of Lu Buwei, Jing Ke and Meng Tian; and most recently, he has written an overview of the Qin dynasty in *The Cambridge History of China* Vol. 1, (Cambridge, 1986). His insights are gratefully acknowledged.

Since the discovery of Qin Shihuang's buried army, numerous articles on the subject have appeared in such periodicals as *Wenwu* and *Kaogu* (in Chinese), and though we have used a number of them, there seems little point in listing them here. In English, there are several treatments of the subject, for instance, in periodicals such as *Smithsonian* (10:8, 1979) and *Early China* (3:1977). M. Hearn discusses the terracotta army in *The Great Bronze Age of China* (New York, 1980), and there is a good deal of useful information in A. Cotterell, *The First Emperor of China*, (Macmillan, London, 1981). The best summary of recent archeology is Li Xueqin, *Eastern Zhou and Qin Civilizations* (Yale, New Haven, 1985), but a work perhaps too technical for the lay reader.

For specialized subjects, we have used several works. The definitive work on Qin law, for instance, is A.F.P. Hulsewe, *Remnants of Ch'in Law* (Brill, Leiden, 1985), and for political philosophy, the best source is K.C. Hsiao, *A History of Chinese Political Thought* (Princeton, 1979). J. Needham's magisterial study, *Science and Civilization in China*, is probably the most important Sinological project of the twentieth century. The first of several volumes was published by Cambridge University Press in 1954, and the work continues. These volumes provide a wealth of information about many aspects of traditional Chinese civilization and were useful to us for their discussion of roads, canals, wall-building and the elixirs of immortality. M. Loewe's various studies of the Han dynasty, which followed the Qin, are of value to anyone interested in early China since the Han period is far better known than the short-lived Qin. K.C. Chang is the editor of an interesting volume called *Food in Chinese Culture* (Yale, New Haven, 1977), and we might also mention Li Yu-ning, *The First Emperor of China*, (New York, 1977). This is an historiographical study of Qin Shihuang, and offers translations of the numerous articles praising him which appeared in China during the 1970s. Cho-yun Hsu's *Ancient China in Transition*, (Stanford, 1965), is an excellent study of society and social mobility during the five centuries prior to the Qin unification.

Finally, in addition to the translations cited above, there are three others of some relevance. H.H. Dubs, *The History of the Former Han Dynasty by Pan Ku*, 3 vols. (Baltimore, 1938, 1944 and 1955) is an excellent source for the rise of the Han. J.J.L. Duyvendak, *The Book of Lord Shang* (London, 1928) studies the life and career of Shang Yang whose reforms set the state of Qin on the road to conquest. J.I. Crump's, *Chan-kuo Ts'e* translates this collection of the diplomatic intrigues of the Warring States Period, including, of course, those of Qin.

We acknowledge gratefully the work of all these authors, and recommend them to the interested reader. Any errors in this text are those of the present authors.

ILLUSTRATION & PHOTO CREDITS

圖　片　説　明

The following abbreviations are used:

CMA: The Cleveland Museum of Art, Cleveland, Ohio
Freer: The Freer Gallery of Art, Smithsonian Institution, Washington, D.C.
NAMA: Nelson-Atkins Museum of Art, Kansas City, Missouri
ROM: The Royal Ontario Museum, Toronto, Canada

endpapers: Chavannes, Edouard. *Mission Archéologique dans la Chine Septentrionale*. (Paris, 1909)
1: ROM
10-11: Chavannes
12: *Sancai tuhui*
14: *Wenwu*
15: ROM
17: Kürschner, Joseph. *China* (1901)
20: *Sancai tuhui*
21: *Shiji*, 1881 reprint
22: *Sancai tuhui*
23: ROM
24-25: NAMA
26: ROM
26-27: ROM
27: ROM
28: ROM
29: ROM
30-31: ROM
32: Cultural Relics Bureau, Beijing
33: Freer, Chinese painting, Yuan, by Qian Xuan, ca 1235-after 1300. Yang Guifei mounting a horse, 57.14
34: Cultural Relics Bureau, Beijing
35: *Mémoires concernant l'histoire, les sciences, les arts... de Chinois*. Paris, 1780, t. 12
37: Cultural Relics Bureau, Beijing
38-39: Chavannes
39: ROM
40-41: Chavannes
42: Cultural Relics Bureau, Beijing

45: Wan-go Weng/National Palace Museum
46: Wan-go Weng/National Palace Museum
48: Cultural Relics Bureau, Beijing
49: Freer, 54.21 D
50: Lair, H.P. and Wang, L.C. (trans). *An Illustrated Life of Confucius*. (Taipei, 1972)
51: ROM
55: left: ROM
right: Freer, Chinese bronze: Late Zhou dynasty. Warring States Period. Chariot (?) fitting, 32.15, 32.16
56: Cultural Relics Bureau, Beijing
57: lower: Cultural Relics Bureau, Beijing
upper: ROM
58: lower: Cultural Relics Bureau, Beijing
upper: *Wenwu*
59: lower: Metropolitan Museum of Art
upper: *Wenwu*
60: Robert Harding Picture Library
61: Cultural Relics Bureau, Beijing/Metropolitan Museum of Art
62: Cultural Relics Bureau, Beijing
63: *Wenwu*
65: ROM
66: Cultural Relics Bureau, Beijing
67: ROM
69: ROM
72: Cultural Relics Bureau, Beijing/Metropolitan Museum of Art
73: ROM
80: Geil William E. *The Great Wall of China*. (London, 1909)
81: Wan-go Weng/National Palace Museum
82-83: Chavannes
84-85: E.T. Archive/National Palace Museum, Taiwan
87: Chavannes
90: *Sancai tuhui*
92: ROM
93: ROM
94: *Mémoires...*
95: CMA, Mr. and Mrs. William H. Marlatt Fund, 61.89
96: *An Illustrated Life of Confucius*
97: C. Pagani
98-99: *Oryun Hgengsil*
101: ROM
103: ROM
105: CMA, John L. Severance Fund, 79.27 a
106: *Sancai tuhui*

107:        ROM
108:        *Historical Relics Unearthed in New China*,
            Beijing, 1972.
109:        Freer, 54.21 B
111:        *Oryun Hgengsil*
112-113:   Chavannes
116-117:   Cultural Relics Bureau, Beijing
118-119:   Wan-go Weng/National Palace Museum
119:        *Free China Review* (vol. 38 no. 10)
123:        ROM
125:        Chavannes
128:        ROM
129:        Freer, Chinese lacquer: 4th-3rd cent. B.C.
            Late Zhou dynasty, Warring States period.
            From Changsha, 57.14
130:        Robert Harding Picture Library
131:        left: Cultural Relics Bureau, Beijing
            right: ROM
            bottom: Robert Harding Picture Library
132-133:   NAMA
135:        E.T. Archive/Bibliotheque Nationale, Paris
136:        ROM
137:        Chavannes
138-139:   ROM
141:        ROM
142-143:   D & J Heaton/Miller Comstock Ltd.
145:        upper: Werner Forman Archive/
            National Palace Museum
            lower: Warren Gordon/Miller Comstock Inc.
146:        Cultural Relics Bureau, Beijing
148:        ©1980 by Arnoldo Mondadori Editore, Milan
149:        ROM
155:        Museum of the Xianyang, Shaanxi
156-157:   James Hsu/ROM
158-159:   Chavannes
162:        ROM
163:        CMA, The Fanny Tewksbury King Collection,
            56.709
167:        E.T. Archive/Bibliotheque Nationale, Paris
168:        Chavannes, E. *Journal Asiatique*
169:        NAMA
170-171:   Chavannes
173:        Giraudon
174-175:   Cultural Relics Bureau, Beijing
176:        Geil, William E. *The Great Wall of China*.
            (New York, 1909)
180:        Cultural Relics Bureau, Beijing/

            Metropolitan Museum of Art
185:        Cultural Relics Bureau, Beijing/
            Metropolitan Museum of Art
187:        Cultural Relics Bureau, Beijing
188:        *Sancai tuhui*
189:        ROM
190-191:   Chavannes
192-193:   James Acland Slide Collection/
            Far Eastern Dept., ROM
196:        ROM
198:        ROM
            Cultural Relics Bureau, Beijing
201:        Bridgeman Art Library/British Museum
203:        ROM

All maps and the line drawing of the palace on pp. 153-154
by Fortunato Aglialoro.

*Photographs courtesy of The National Film Board of Canada
on pp. 12-13, 30-31, 42-43, 52-53, 54, 64-65, 68, 70-71, 74-75,
76-77, 88-89, 114-115, 117, 126-127, 147, 149, 150, 151, 152-153,
160-161, 164-165, 166, 177, 180-181, 182-183, 184, 186, 204-205.*

Index

A

Afang Palace, 16, 127, 154, 168
"All Under Heaven", 47, 86, 89, 132, 140
Analects, The, 98, 99, 100
armour, Qin, 62-63
Art of War, 47
Art of War, The, 102

B

ba-shen ("Eight Spirits"), 139
Bai Qi, 64
Blessed Isles of the Eastern Sea, 142
Bodde, D., 22
Book of History, 165
Book of Odes, 128, 165
books, burned, 197
books, burning of, 16, 100, 130, 134, 146, 168, 200, 207
buried army, 55, 56, 178, 207

C

Cambridge History of China, The, 200
China's First Unifier, 22

Chinese Classics, 95, 96, 97, 99
Chu, army of, 51, 70
Chu, state of, 36, 47, 52, 78, 104, 130
Classic of Music, The, 131
Classics. See Chinese Classics
concubines, 20, 33, 102, 130, 172, 178
Confucianism, 20, 98, 135, 201
Confucians, 134, 173, 196, 202
Confucius, 51, 94, 95, 97, 98, 99, 100, 102, 104, 106, 108, 111, 127, 130, 135, 138, 168
conscription, army, 55, 64, 156, 199
conscription, labour, 106, 112, 122, 134, 146, 165, 196, 197

D

daughter of Yao, 136
diviners, 70
Dragon Throne, 14
Dujiang Weir canal, 145
Duke Mu, 29, 94
Duke of Qi, 96
Duke of Qin, 48
Duke Xiao, 48

E

Eastern Isles, 25, 203
elixir of immortality, 25, 132, 142, 154, 166, 173, 174, 203
eunuchs, 118, 119, 172

F

Fan Sui, 64
feudalism, 44, 46, 48, 204
feudalism, abolition of, 88-89, 134
Five Elements, the theory of, 86, 138
Five Phases, the theory of.

See Five Elements, the theory of
Five Tortures, the, 37
"Five Vermin of the State", the, 111
"Four Gods", 138
Fu Su, 166, 174

G

Gaozu, 188, 189, 200, 201, 202, 203, 205
God of the Yang force, 139
gong (Duke), 28
Great Wall, the, 16, 26, 47, 76, 80, 112, 144, 146, 148, 156, 165, 166, 174, 196, 197, 206

H

Han dynasty, 88, 89, 119, 135, 140, 186, 188, 200, 201, 205
Han Feizi, 92, 108, 110, 111, 112
Han, state of, 47, 78, 145
Han Wudi, 202, 203, 204
Handan, 33, 78
herbs of immortality. See elixir of immortality
"High Progenitor". See Gaozu
"Hu", (Xiongnu barbarians), 162
Hu Hai, 36, 37, 118, 172, 174, 176, 178, 186, 194, 195, 196
Huan I, 78
huangdi (Duke), 86, 143, 201
huangdi (emperor), 14
hun, 140
"Hundred Flowers". See "Hundred Schools"
"Hundred Schools", the, 92, 108, 195

I

Imperial System, 14
inscriptions, 26, 80, 100, 138, 198

Island of the Immortals, 143, 166
Islands of Penglai, 132, 173

J

jade, 26, 27, 32, 70, 172
Jia Yi, 14, 80, 195
jian-yu-shi (an Imperial Overseer or Inspector), 89
Jin, state of, 52, 76
Jing Ke, 38, 39, 78

K

Kangxi dictionary, the, 91
Kansu, province of, 126
keng (live burial), 166
King of Chu, 188
King Fuxi, 90
King Hui, 29
King Wen, 154
King Wu, 29, 154
King Yao, 142
King Zhaoxiang, 29
Kong Fuzi. See Confucius

L

Land of Immortals, 142, 143
Langyai, 132, 139, 156, 173
Lao Ai, 34, 36, 77
Lao Zi, 104, 138
Legalism, 20, 108, 110, 111, 112, 116, 134, 164, 194, 201, 202
Li River, 145
Li Si, 16, 22, 24, 29, 36, 74, 78, 88, 89, 90, 108, 110, 162, 164, 168, 172, 174, 176, 186, 194
Liji, 128
Lord of Chu. See Xiang Yu
Lord of the Four Seasons, 139
Lord of Han. See Gaozu
Lord of the Sun, 139
Lu, state of, 94, 96, 97, 127
Lu Buwei, 16, 32, 33, 34, 36, 77, 140
Luoyang, 44

M
Machiavelli, Nicolo, 110
Magister Lu, 162, 168
Mao Tse-tung, 14
Mencius, 106
Meng I, 118
Meng Ao, 77
Meng Tian, 77, 80, 90, 118, 144, 146, 156
Ming dynasty, 119
Mo Zi, 98, 102, 104
Mongolia, 144
mother of Shihuang. See Zhao Ji
Mount Cheng, 139
Mount Li, 55, 127, 154, 156, 176, 178
Mount Tai, 127, 132, 138, 203

N
nine sacred bronze tripods, 136

P
"Pivot of Heaven". See Afang Palace
po, 140
Polo, Marco, 148
"Practice", 99-100

Q
Qi, state of, 44, 47, 72, 78, 86, 96, 97
Qin dynasty, 16, 22, 36, 92, 112, 125, 130, 134, 164, 188, 195, 196, 200, 201

R
Records of the Historian. See Shiji
ren (humanity or benevolence), 98
Rong, the, 28, 44

S
scholars, execution of, 16, 146, 207

search for immortality, 142-143, 172-173, 203, 140. See also elixir of immortality
Second Emperor, the. See Hu Hai
"seven methods", the, 110
Shandong, 138
Shang dynasty, 47, 72
Shang Yang, 48, 49, 64, 74, 108, 112
Shiji, 20, 22, 24, 26, 27, 31, 32, 34, 36, 47, 51, 53, 55, 70, 75, 76, 80, 81, 86, 88, 90, 94, 96, 119, 140, 144, 154, 155, 156, 162, 166, 170, 173, 176, 178, 186, 189, 195, 204
shou (a Civil Governor), 89
Shun, 173
Sima Qian, 20, 195, 204
Sins of Qin, The, 14, 195
Spring and Autumn Period, 50, 51, 52
standardization, 16, 36, 48, 90, 91, 130, 205
Sun Zi, 47, 102

T
Tang dynasty, 119
Tao, the, 98, 100, 104
Taoism, 104, 134, 202
Tian Dan of Qi, 53
tomb of Shihuang, 16, 47, 55, 56, 64, 130, 154, 156, 168, 176, 178, 188

U
UNESCO's 1950 Statement on Race, 98
unification of China, 78, 80, 138, 204

W
Wang Guan, 88
wang (King), 29
Wang Qian, 78

Wan (ten-thousand), 148
Warring States Period, the, 31, 47, 51, 53, 55, 81, 146
Warring States, the, 14, 24, 27, 48, 86
Warriors, Qin, 58-63
Way, the. See Tao, the
Weapons, Qin, 66-69
wei (a Military Governor), 89
Wei Liao, 22
Wei River Valley, 186, 188
Wei, state of, 46, 48, 64, 77, 78, 81
wei-wu-wei (do nothing and nothing will not be done), 104, 202
wen (writing), 91
wen-hua (culture), 91
wen-ming (civilization), 91
Wuhan, 112

X
Xia dynasty, 47
Xi'an, 28, 55
Xiang River, 145
Xiang Yu, 186, 188, 189
Xianyang, 16, 28, 37, 44, 88, 127, 144, 154, 174, 186, 188, 195, 196, 197
Xiongnu, 111, 156, 202
Xu Shi, 143
Xun Zi, 36, 74, 106, 108
xun-shou (tours), 138

Y
Yan, army of, 51, 53
Yan, state of, 38, 47, 53, 78
Yang force, the, 104
Yangtze River, 136, 170, 178, 186
Yellow Emperor, 91
Yellow River, 186
Yin force, the, 104, 139
"Yu the Great", 47, 173
Yue, 162

Z
Zhao, army of, 55
Zhao Gao, 118, 172, 174, 176, 186, 194
Zhao Ji, 16, 24, 32, 33, 34, 35, 78, 99, 140
Zhao, state of, 32, 33, 46, 48, 64, 75, 77, 78
Zhengguo canal, 145
zhenren ("Pure Being"), 104
Zhou dynasty. See Zhou, the house of
Zhou, the House of, 28, 44, 47, 86, 87, 88, 94, 106, 136
Zhuang Zi, 104
Zi Ying, 176, 186, 188
Zizhu, 32
Zou Yan, 138
Zuozuan, 52